Fodor's
25 Best

FLORENCE

How to Use This Book

KEY TO SYMBOLS

✚ Map reference to the accompanying fold-out map

✉ Address

☎ Telephone number

🕓 Opening/closing times

🍴 Restaurant or café

🚊 Nearest rail station

🚌 Nearest bus route

⛴ Nearest riverboat or ferry stop

♿ Facilities for visitors with disabilities

❓ Other practical information

▷ Further information

ℹ Tourist information

✋ Admission charges: Expensive (over €10), Moderate (€5–€10), and Inexpensive (under €5)

This guide is divided into four sections

● Essential Florence: An introduction to the city and tips on making the most of your stay.
● Florence by Area: We've broken the city into four areas, and recommended the best sights, shops, entertainment venues, nightlife and places to eat in each one. Suggested walks help you to explore on foot.
● Where to Stay: The best hotels, whether you're looking for luxury, budget or something in between.
● Need to Know: The info you need to make your trip run smoothly, including getting about by public transport, weather tips, emergency phone numbers and useful websites.

Navigation In the Florence by Area chapter, we've given each area its own colour, which is also used on the locator maps throughout the book and the map on the inside front cover.

Maps The fold-out map with this book is a comprehensive street plan of Florence. The grid on this fold-out map is the same as the grid on the locator maps within the book. We've given grid references within the book for each sight and listing.

Contents

CONTENTS

Introducing Florence

Florence is one of the world's greatest art destinations, its famous museums, galleries, churches, palazzi and piazzas all crowded into a ravishing, compact *centro storico*. There's more to this historic gem than its art treasures, however: fashionistas, foodies and fans of the good life will not leave disappointed.

Shoppers here will find everything from chic designer shops and bespoke shoemakers to market stalls touting bargain leather goods and cheap jewellery. Florence's artisan tradition goes back centuries, and despite the pressures of the modern economy, you can still find furniture restorers and picture framers plying their trade in tiny workshops in the Oltrarno area of the city.

The thriving food and drink culture embraces everything from hole-in-the-wall wine bars and tripe stands to family-run trattorias and white-cloth gourmet establishments, while new cocktail bars are opening all the time.

Florence is more visitor-friendly than ever and large areas of the *centro storico* are now traffic-free.

Museums have been revamped, there is a modern opera house and work on the much-awaited (albeit controversial) tram system is nearing completion. A younger, more energetic vibe is challenging the city's once-staid image of a living museum.

This is a city where blockbuster sights attract millions each year, so try to visit out of season (in the winter). If you can't avoid the crowds, seek out the lesser sights, many of which are hugely rewarding, and leave plenty of time for aimless wandering through cobbled backstreets and quiet piazzas. When it all gets too much, head out to the hills of Chianti for a breath of fresh air: this iconic, rolling landscape of vineyards, olive groves and cypress trees is right on the doorstep.

FACTS AND FIGURES

● Florence attracts around 7 million visitors a year.
● Florence has one of the lowest birth rates in Italy.
● The Uffizi Gallery is Italy's most visited museum—with some 2.2 million visitors coming every year.
● In Italian the city is Firenze, but the original Roman settlement was called Florentia.

UNCHANGED FLORENCE

Today's visitors experience a city that has changed little since the first tourists arrived in the 18th century. The cityscape is still dominated by the dome of the Duomo, the majority of the artistic treasures are still in their original places, tourists still heavily outnumber Florentines and, most surprisingly of all, the richest Florentine families today are the same as they were in 1427.

ON THE BALL

The Medici family, virtual sovereigns from the 14th to 18th centuries, left their mark on every building connected with them, so look out for their coat of arms, a varying number of balls *(palle)* on a shield, on buildings everywhere. The *palle* probably represent pills or coins, references to the family's original trade as apothecaries and later their role as bankers.

FLOOD FACTS

In November 1966 the River Arno burst its banks to disastrous effect: the tide, bludgeoning through the streets, reached as high as 6m (20ft) in the Santa Croce neighbourhood. This was not the only flood there has ever been, however: bridges were swept away in 1269 and 1333, and the city was submerged in 1557 and 1884, but not as badly as in 1966.

A Short Stay in Florence

DAY 1

Morning After breakfast head to the **Duomo** (▷ 58–59) and prepare to be awed by its mighty proportions; alongside are the superb **Campanile** (▷ 56) and **Battistero** (▷ 54–55). You can find out more about the history at the nearby **Museo dell'Opera del Duomo** (▷ 62). If you are feeling fit and don't suffer from vertigo, climb to the top of either the Duomo or Campanile for great views of the city.

Mid-morning Order a coffee at one of the café-terraces that line the traffic-free Piazza del Duomo to recharge your batteries. Head northwest up to **Mercato San Lorenzo** (▷ 68), the street market that now sprawls around the **Mercato Centrale** building (▷ 68). Traders here sell everything from knitwear to jewellery. It's known for its bargain leather goods, but keep a look out for pickpockets and don't be afraid to haggle.

Lunch Opposite the northern flank of San Lorenzo church is the unassuming **Sergio Gozzi** (▷ 76), renowned for its Florentine cooking.

Afternoon Finish your shopping and then walk down Via dei Pucci and right into Via Ricasoli to the **Galleria dell'Accademia** (▷ 60–61) to view Michelangelo's massive masterpiece, *David*. There's plenty more to see in the gallery, or you might prefer to backtrack and take in the Chapel of the Magi in **Palazzo Medici-Riccardi** (▷ 63).

Dinner For a special treat book a table at the **Winter Garden by Caino** (▷ 50). A cheaper option is **Belle Donne** (▷ 47), located close to **Via de' Tornabuoni** (▷ 36).

Evening Stroll down to the grandiose **Piazza della Repubblica** (▷ 39), with its triumphal arch, for a touch of Florentine atmosphere.

DAY 2

Morning Queues form from as early as 7am at the **Galleria degli Uffizi** (▷ 28–29), with its priceless paintings and sculptures, so book ahead online via the official website and allow a whole morning for your visit.

Lunch After you've seen all you want at the Uffizi, splash out and relax with a coffee on the terrace of historic **Rivoire** (▷ 50), the most elegant café on **Piazza della Signoria** (▷ 32). Alternatively, if you fancy something more substantial, tuck into hearty Tuscan cuisine at **Dei Frescobaldi** (▷ 48) on the opposite side of the square. Leave the piazza by its southwest corner, heading down Via Por Santa Maria, and stroll over the **Ponte Vecchio** (▷ 34–35) to be dazzled by its jewellery shops. There are plenty more gift shops just over the bridge.

Afternoon Take in the **Palazzo Pitti** (▷ 84–85). There are seven museums, plus the Royal Apartments to see, but if the weather is hot, you might prefer to stroll in the **Giardino di Boboli** (▷ 82). Palazzo Pitti is very popular, so be prepared to wait or book in advance. Then wander along to the church of Santa Maria del Carmine with the **Cappella Brancacci** (▷ 81) and its wonderful frescoes. The area is full of artisan workshops, boutiques and cafés and bars. If you are not tired, cross over Ponte Santa Trinita and walk along the riverfront to **Santa Croce** (▷ 33).

Dinner The Boccadama (▷ 47) wine bar-cum-restaurant is in a nice spot to appreciate the lively square of Santa Croce.

Evening If the weather is kind you can get a great view of the city after dark from **Piazzale Michelangelo** (▷ 87) in the southeast of Oltrarno. Catch bus 13 to get there. Alternatively, take bus 7 up to the hill town of **Fiesole** (▷ 97) for wonderful views of Florence illuminated at night.

Top 25

ESSENTIAL FLORENCE TOP 25

▶ ▶ ▶

Bargello ▷ 24–25 An overview of Florentine sculpture through works by Michelangelo and others.

Battistero ▷ 54–55 One of Florence's oldest buildings, famous for its mosaics and bronze doors.

Campanile ▷ 56 An incredible sight towering 85m (279ft) over the city, and offering great views.

Via de' Tornabuoni ▷ 36 The cream of world fashion is elegantly displayed on this street in the heart of medieval Florence.

Santissima Annunziata ▷ 67 Elegant, neoclassical arches grace the facade of this lovely church built by Michelozzo.

Santa Maria Novella ▷ 66 A great Dominican church with an exquisite facade.

Santa Croce ▷ 33 The largest Franciscan church in Italy, incorporating the Cappella dei Pazzi. Galileo and Michelangelo are buried here.

San Miniato al Monte ▷ 83 A fine Romanesque church perched on a hill with wonderful views.

San Marco ▷ 65 Beautiful convent where the paintings of Fra Angelico are a feast for the eyes.

San Lorenzo ▷ 64 This church is a superb example of archetypal Renaissance architecture.

Ponte Vecchio ▷ 34–35 One of the immediately recognizable emblems of Florence.

Piazza della Signoria ▷ 32 A traffic-free open-air sculpture gallery surrounded by elegant cafés.

Le Cascine

Arno

SAN FREDIANO

BELLOSGUARDO

NORTH CENTRO 51–76

SAN GIOVANNI

SANTA MARIA NOVELLA

Santa Maria Novella

Palazzo Medici-Riccardi

Cappelle Medicee

San Lorenzo

Duomo

Battistero

Campanile

Via de' Tornabuoni

Palazzo Vecchio

Piazza della Signoria

SANTO SPIRITO

Galleria degli Uffizi

Cappella Brancacci

Ponte Vecchio

Museo Galileo

Giardino Torrigiani

Palazzo Pitti

Giardino di Boboli

Fonte del Nettuno

OLTRARNO 77–92

BOBOLINO

These pages are a quick guide to the Top 25, which are described in more detail later. Here they are listed alphabetically, and the tinted background shows which area they are in.

Cappella Brancacci
▷ **80–81** The chapel is famous for its monumental fresco cycle.

Cappella dei Pazzi ▷ **26**
An early Renaissance masterpiece by Filippo Brunelleschi.

Cappelle Medicee ▷ **57**
The Medici family's tombs and private chapels, visible proof of their wealth.

Duomo ▷ **58–59** A sublime masterpiece of Renaissance architecture topped by a mighty dome.

Fiesole ▷ **97** The perfect hilltop destination for a change from the city and its crowds.

Galleria dell'Accademia ▷ **60–61** Home to *David*, Michelangelo's world-famous sculpture.

Galleria degli Uffizi ▷ **28–29** The most important collection of Renaissance art anywhere.

Giardino di Boboli ▷ **82** A green space in the middle of Florence and a cool oasis on a hot summer's day.

Museo Galileo ▷ **27** The history of science brought to life with this fine collection.

Museo dell'Opera del Duomo ▷ **62** Museum housing sculpture from the Duomo and Baptistery.

Palazzo Medici-Riccardi ▷ **63** The residence of the Medici until 1540.

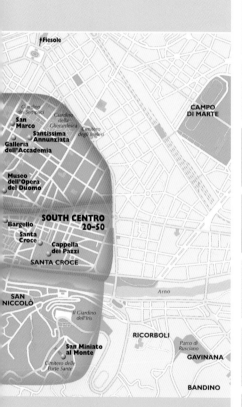

Palazzo Vecchio ▷ **30**
The grand 14th-century embodiment of Florentine civic purposes.

Palazzo Pitti ▷ **84–85**
The city's largest and most opulent palace, containing a fine picture collection.

Shopping

Florence may be small, but its shopping scene packs a punch. This little city has it all and holds an advantage over larger rivals Milan and Rome in that it is easily accessible on foot. Italians and visitors alike dive into the heady mix of chic designer stores and bargain market stalls, quirky boutiques, independent fashion ateliers and artisan workshops. Gastronomes will be impressed by the variety of food and wine on offer at rival outlets Eataly (▷ 71) and the top floor of the Mercato Centrale (▷ 68), converted in 2015, but also intrigued by tiny grocer's shops and *gastronomie* (delicatessen) in residential neighbourhoods where the locals do their daily shopping.

Something to Take Home

The nicest souvenirs are often everyday items—kitchenware, household linen, tools and stationery. Head for the San Lorenzo market area for good-value espresso coffee-makers and the tiny cups to go with them, wonderful gadgets such as fish-scalers, and plastic utensils in vivid shades. Inexpensive, cheerful children's toys also make good gifts; the tiny shops away from the main streets often offer the best value. Fresh produce and leather goods are also in plentiful supply in Florence's markets. Food is a popular take-home; aside from expensive olive oil and local wine, don't overlook more prosaic items such as dried herbs specially blended for different foods, the excellent stock cubes known as *dadi* or sachets of vanilla sugar.

STREET TRADE

Street trading is part of the Florentine scene, as in all major Italian cities, with tourists being offered everything from fake designer bags to African objects. However, most traders are unlicensed and keep a constant eye open for approaching *carabinieri*, ready to scoop up their merchandise and run. Be aware the authorities take a dim view of such practices and purchasers can be heavily fined for buying counterfeit goods.

Florence is the place to shop for shoes, designer names, leather goods and culinary delights

Traditional Crafts

One of Florence's more unusual attractions is the wealth of artisan workshops, clustered mainly across the river in the bohemian Oltrarno area. Many specialize in antiques restoration for the city's numerous dealers, but there are others engaging in more everyday activities. Look for picture framers where you can get new purchases mounted, shoemakers selling wonderful velvet pads and brushes, and book binders where you may have a chance to watch the whole creative process.

Florence on View

Prints, books and old maps and city plans make special souvenirs. Another good option is a cookbook on Tuscan cuisine, readily available in English. Beautiful calendars with views of Florence are on sale as early as April for the following year. The museum shops are good for these, too. Via Maggio and Via de' Fossi are lined with venerable antiques shops with interesting treasures in the windows.

Florentine Kitsch

There's no chance that you'll be overwhelmed by good taste either; there are T-shirts bearing images of Michelangelo and Botticelli, plastic models of the Duomo and Ponte Vecchio, umbrellas shaped like the Duomo, grotesque ceramics and fakes of every description. Where else could you buy such a garish silvery reproduction of Michelangelo's *David*, complete with twinkling lights?

Something to take home—a designer garment from Pucci, local produce or Florentine paper

ON A BUDGET

Markets are generally a good source of budget and second-hand clothing. The Cascine market (▷ 98), held each Tuesday morning, is where locals go for bargains. The area around San Lorenzo is a great place for up-to-the-minute, inexpensive designs. The Mall (☎ 055 865 7775; firenze.themall.it), a 30-minute drive south of Florence at Leccio, has outlets for all the top designer brands (twice daily bus from Florence central bus station).

ESSENTIAL FLORENCE SHOPPING

Shopping by Theme

Whether you're looking for a department store, a quirky boutique, or something in between, you'll find it all in Florence. On this page stores are listed by theme. For a more detailed write-up, see the individual listings in Florence by Area.

Antiques and Prints

Baccani (▷ 41)
Bartolozzi & Maioli (▷ 89)
Bottega delle Stampe (▷ 89)
La Casa della Stampa (▷ 89)
Cornici Campani (▷ 71)
Vanda Nencioni (▷ 45)

Ceramics and Homeware

Armando Poggi (▷ 41)
Bartolini (▷ 71)
La Botteghina del Ceramista (▷ 71)
Moleria Locchi (▷ 90)
Pampaloni (▷ 44)
Richard Ginori (▷ 73)
Sbigoli Terrecotte (▷ 73)

Department Stores

Coin (▷ 42)
La Rinascente (▷ 44)

Fashion

Anichini (▷ 41)
Anna (▷ 89)
Emilio Cavallini (▷ 42)
Emilio Pucci (▷ 42)
Florence Factory (▷ 42)
Intimissimi (▷ 72)
J. T. Casini ▷ (89)
Luisa Via Roma (▷ 43)
Société Anonyme (▷ 73)

Food and Drink

Alessi (▷ 71)
Casa del Vino (▷ 71)
Eataly (▷ 71)
Enoteca Peri (▷ 89)
Olio & Convivium (▷ 90)
Olivia (▷ 92)
Osteria de l'Ortolano (▷ 72)
Pegna (▷ 44)
Sforno (▷ 90)
Vestri (▷ 73)
Zanobini (▷ 73)

Health, Beauty and Perfume

Aquaflor (▷ 41)
Dr Vranjes (▷ 71)
Officina Profumo-Farmaceutica di Santa Maria Novella (▷ 43)
Olfattorio (▷ 43–44)

Jewellery

Angela Caputi (▷ 41)
Cassetti (▷ 42)
Fratelli Piccini (▷ 42)
Parenti (▷ 44)
Penko Bottega Orafa (▷ 72)
Sara Amrhein (▷ 90)

Leather and Shoes

Benheart (▷ 41)
Il Bisonte (▷ 41)
Cellerini (▷ 42)
Furla (▷ 43)
Leather School of Santa Croce (▷ 43)
Madova Gloves (▷ 90)
Martelli (▷ 43)
Misuri (▷ 43)
Otisopse (▷ 44)
Rive Gauche (▷ 90)
Salvatore Ferragamo (▷ 45)
Stefano Bemer (▷ 90)

Linen and Fabrics

Antico Setificio Fiorentino (▷ 89)
Frette (▷ 72)
Loretta Caponi (▷ 72)
Valmar (▷ 45)

Stationery, Books and Gifts

Alice's Masks Art Studio (▷ 71)
Feltrinelli (▷ 42)
Giulio Giannini e Figlio (▷ 89)
Letizia Fiorini (▷ 43)
Libreria Antiquaria Gonnelli (▷ 72)
Mandragora Artstore (▷ 72)
Il Papiro (▷ 72)
Parione (▷ 44)
Le Pietre Nell'Arte (▷ 73)
Pineider (▷ 44)
Scriptorium (▷ 73)
Il Torchio (▷ 90)

Florence by Night

To kick off your evening and for a taste of local life don't miss the *passeggiata*. This quintessentially Italian nightly ritual sees the streets thronged with locals, out to see and be seen, while window-shopping, meeting friends and eating *gelato*.

An Evening Stroll
The best place to see the fashion peacocks in their finery is on Via dei Calzaiuoli, linking Piazza del Duomo with Piazza della Signoria. To enjoy a drink while you people-watch, try one of the cafés in Piazza della Repubblica, but be prepared to pay a hefty supplement for sitting outside. After dinner, stroll along the Lungarni, the streets that run beside the river. The Ponte Vecchio is just as crowded by night as by day.

Stunning by Night
Evening is the ideal time to admire Florentine architecture as the floodlighting enhances many buildings. Don't miss the Piazza della Signoria and the area between it and the Duomo. The private palazzi look superb at this time of day and you can peek into courtyards and loggias.

Culture, Concerts and Clubbing
Florence has a year-round schedule of cultural events. The excellent, bi-weekly *The Florentine* (theflorentine.net) is free, in English and has full listings. The monthly *Firenze Spettacolo* (firenzespettacolo.it) also details everything, including rock concerts, clubs and discos.

After dark enjoy a stroll around the city's illuminated buildings and finish with a drink in a historic bar

---

PICK OF THE PANORAMAS

A great evening vantage point is Piazzale Michelangelo (▷ 87), which gives a glorious panorama of the Duomo illuminated, Florence's twinkling lights and the misty hills beyond. The square draws the crowds during the day but things are quieter at night. There's a restaurant and a couple of bars if you want to spend the evening here, but avoid the park/gardens area below the square at night. In late June, the square hosts the spectacular fireworks display celebrating the feast of San Giovanni.

Where to Eat

Eating is definitely one of life's pleasures in Florence, as it is all over Italy. The food is fresh, seasonal and, above all, local. You'll eat the best of Tuscan produce cooked to Tuscan recipes.

Mealtimes

If you are heading for breakfast in a bar, most open for business around 7–7.30. Restaurants normally open for lunch around 12.30 or 1 and stop serving at 3; they close for the afternoon and reopen for dinner around 7.30. The majority of restaurants close one day a week but many open every day in summer.

Trattoria or Osteria?

Trattorie are usually family-run places and are generally more basic than restaurants. Sometimes there is no written menu and the waiter will reel off the list of the day's specials. The food and surroundings in a *ristorante* are usually more refined, and prices will reflect this. *Pizzerie* specialize in pizzas, but often serve other dishes as well. Look out for establishments advertising *forno al legno*—a wood-fired oven. *Osterie* can either be old-fashioned places specializing in home-cooked food or extremely elegant, long-established restaurants. All categories will add a bread and cover charge, which will vary from around €2 to a whopping €5 or €6 in the most refined places; a service charge will often be added as well.

PAYING THE BILL

Pay by requesting the bill (*il conto*), and check to see whether service is included. Scribbled bills on scraps of paper are illegal; if you don't get a proper one, say that you need a receipt (*una recevuta*), which all restaurants, bars and shops are legally obliged to issue. Both they and you can be fined if you do not take this with you. Some smaller establishments expect to be paid in cash but you'll be able to use a credit card in most places. Even if service is included, it's customary to leave a small tip—some loose change will do.

Italian cuisine Florentine-style. Nothing beats a drink or an ice cream outside on a sunny piazza

Where to Eat by Cuisine

There are plenty of places to eat to suit all tastes and budgets in Florence. On this page they are listed by cuisine. For a more detailed description of each restaurant, see Florence by Area.

Cafés
Caffè Amerini (▷ 47)
Gilli (▷ 49)
Giubbe Rosse (▷ 49)
Paszkowski (▷ 49)
Rivoire (▷ 50)
Robiglio (▷ 76)

Cheap Eats
Al Tranvai (▷ 91)
Ara: è Sud (▷ 46)
La Casalinga (▷ 92)
De' Benci (▷ 48)
Del Fagioli (▷ 48)
Lorenzo Nigro—Il
   Lampredotto (▷ 76)
Olivia (▷ 92)
Sergio Gozzi (▷ 76)

Good for *Bistecca*
Cammillo (▷ 92)
Le Cave di Maiano
   (▷ 105)
Il Fiesolano (Perseus)
   (▷ 105)
Il Latini (▷ 49)

Good for Vegetarians and Pescatarians
Antellesi (▷ 75)
Belle Donne (▷ 47)

Burro e Acciughe (▷ 91)
Povero Pesce (▷ 106)
Santo Spirito (▷ 92)

Gourmet Dining
Belcore (▷ 75)
Il Cibrèo (▷ 47)
Enoteca Pinchiorri (▷ 48)
La Giostra (▷ 76)
La Loggia (▷ 106)
La Ménagère (▷ 76)
Sabatini (▷ 76)
Il Santo Bevitore (▷ 92)
SE.STO on Arno (▷ 50)
Winter Garden by Caino
   (▷ 50)

Ice Cream
La Carraia (▷ 47)
Gelateria Carabé (▷ 75)
Perché No! (▷ 49)
Vivoli (▷ 50)

International
Dim Sum (▷ 48)
Kome (▷ 49)
Ruth's (▷ 76)

Pizza
L'Antica Pizzeria da
   Michele (▷ 75)

Baldovino (▷ 46)
La Bussola (▷ 47)
Il Pizzaiuolo (▷ 49)

Typical Tuscan
13 Gobbi (▷ 46)
Boccadama (▷ 47)
Cantinetta Antinori
   (▷ 75)
Coco Lezzone (▷ 48)
Del Carmine (▷ 92)
Le Mossacce (▷ 76)
Sostanza (▷ 50)
Zà-Zà (▷ 76)

Wine Bars
Cantinetta dei Verrazzano
   (▷ 47)
Coquinarius (▷ 75)
Dei Frescobaldi (▷ 48)
Fuori Porta (▷ 106)
Procacci (▷ 50)
Le Volpi e l'Uva (▷ 92)

Top Tips For...

These great suggestions will help you tailor your ideal visit to Florence, no matter how you choose to spend your time. Each suggestion has a fuller write-up elsewhere in the book.

EXCLUSIVE SHOPPING

Head to Via de' Tornabuoni (▷ 36) for the best in designer names—Armani, Gucci, Prada and local designer Roberto Cavalli.

All that glitters is indeed gold in the little shops that line the Ponte Vecchio (▷ 34–35), and prices are competitive too.

Florence is famed for its superb shoes, and one of the best brands is Salvatore Ferragamo (▷ 45); you can visit the museum, too (▷ 38).

TAKING A SOUVENIR HOME

Stationery—Pineider (▷ 44) has a fabulous array of handmade paper, notebooks and desk accessories. For traditional Florentine paper, try Il Torchio (▷ 90).

Ceramics—choose an authentic jug or plate at Sbigoli Terrecotte (▷ 73).

Wine—Casa del Vino (▷ 71) stocks wines from Tuscany and beyond in all price ranges.

SAMPLING THE LOCAL CUISINE

Sit at a shared table, trying out local dishes, at Il Latini (▷ 49).

The cuisine is Tuscan, the restaurant traditional—try Coco Lezzone (▷ 48) for that classic meal.

Not far from the Duomo, down Via del Proconsolo, try Le Mossacce (▷ 76).

HISTORIC CAFÉS

Giubbe Rosse (▷ 49)—watch the world go by in the Piazza della Repubblica.

Paszkowski (▷ 49)—yet more indulgence on the Piazza della Reppublica—try the fruit tarts.

Rivoire (▷ 50)—in the attractive Piazza della Signoria, it's a perfect spot to unwind.

Clockwise from top left: Top shoe designer Salvatore Ferragamo started his business in Florence; Officina Profumo

INDULGING IN ICE CREAM

You'll have difficulty deciding what to choose at Perché No! (▷ 49).

For delicious granitas and their special fruity *cremolata* visit Gelateria Carabé (▷ 75).

The most famous gelateria in Florence, Vivoli (▷ 50), changes its specials to suit the seasons.

A BED IN THE CITY'S HEART

Try the Savoy (▷ 112) for a luxurious oasis of calm right on busy Piazza della Repubblica.

Stylish Via Tornabuoni is home to the Hotel Milu (▷ 111), a boutique designer hotel with incredible service.

Stroll to Santa Maria Novella from Casa Howard (▷ 110), a wonderfully stylish and welcoming hotel.

Enjoy a wonderful city-centre location at a great price at the Hotel Cestelli (▷ 109), just a few minutes' stroll from the Ponte Vecchio.

GREEN SPACES

Tucked away near the university, the tranquil Giardino dei Semplice (▷ 68), with its cool green and medicinal plants, dates from the 16th century.

Escape the heat and crowds to explore the Giardino di Boboli (▷ 82), central Florence's green lung.

Head for the huge, tree-filled space of the Cascine park (▷ 98) to cool off—great for the kids.

PUTTING A SMILE ON THE KIDS' FACES

The Museo Stibbert (▷ 98) has a fine collection of armour for your budding knights.

Go to the soccer stadium (▷ 105) to cheer on local team Fiorentina when they're at home.

If you need to cool off, visit the Piscina le Pavoniere (▷ 105) outdoor pool.

Take the children to the Mercato Nuovo (▷ 37) to see the *Porcellino* and spend their holiday money on a good-value toys, souvenirs or accessories.

sells locally made cosmetics; elegant marbled paper; modern greeting cards; enjoying lunch al fresco

FLORENCE ON A BUDGET

For good value combined with historic surroundings, stay at the Scoti hotel (▷ 109).

If the real thing is a bit pricey, there are great non-designer bargains to be found at San Lorenzo market (▷ 68).

There's no charge to see the stunning paintings in the church of Santa Felicita (▷ 87).

Choose a sunny day for a great walk from the Ponte Vecchio up to Piazzale Michelangelo (▷ 88), with its fabulous views over Florence and the surrounding hills.

THE CITY BY NIGHT

Sip a cocktail at rooftop SE.STO in the Westin Excelsior (▷ 50, 112).

Take a trip up to Piazzale Michelangelo (▷ 87) to view the city in all its glory at night.

Attend a performance at Florence's modern opera house, the Opera di Firenze (▷ 74).

EXPLORING TUSCANY

Head out of town and up the hill to Fiesole (▷ 97), the easiest way to get a taste of Tuscany outside Florence.

Hop on a bus to take in quintessential Tuscan countryside en route to San Gimignano (▷ 103), famous for its towers.

Take the train or bus to Siena (▷ 104), one of Tuscany's most perfect medieval towns.

Plan a trip to historic and beautiful walled Lucca (▷ 100), a prosperous little city that's a superb contrast to the hill towns around Florence.

SOMETHING DIFFERENT

Go for a swim in one of Florence's open-air pools (▷ 105), which are usually set in pleasant, grassy surroundings.

See what the locals buy to eat by browsing the stalls at the Mercato Centrale (▷ 68) or Mercato Sant'Ambrogio (▷ 38).

Be uplifted at a recital in one of Florence's splendid churches such as Santo Stefano al Ponte (▷ 45).

From top: You can browse a market or enjoy the views for free; Boboli Gardens; climb the Duomo for fabulous views

Florence by Area

The South Centro

The heart of historic Florence contains some of the city's most iconic Renaissance palaces, churches and museums. Its largely pedestrianized grid of ancient lanes opens onto wide streets and broad piazzas, home to a plethora of tempting shops.

Top 25

Palazzo
Alessandri
Palazzo
dei Pandolfini
Palazzo Borghese
Bargello
Via della Vigna Vecchia
Via dell' Anguillara
San Firenze
Borgo dei Greci
Palazzo dell'Antella
Piazza
Santa Croce
Teatro G
Verdi
Casa
Buonarroti
VIA GIUSEPPE VERDI
Via dei Pepi
Via del Popolo
Via de' Pandolfini
Via M. Palmieri
Via de' Martiri del
Via Pietrapiana
Sant'
Ambrogio
Via Mattonaia
Borgo la Croce
Piazza
Cesare
Beccaria
Loggia del
Pesce
Piazza
L'Ghiberti
Mercato
Sant'Ambrogio
Via Ferdinando Paolieri
Porta alla
Croce
Facoltà di Arch
(S Verdiana)
ITALIA
Via dell'Agnolo
Via Ghibellina
Via M Buonarroti
Via de' Macci
Le Murate
Archivio
di Stato
Viale
Duca
d'Abruzzi
VIALE GIOVINE
Via de' Conciatori
Ghibellina
Via delle Casine
Via Pietro Thouar
Borgo S Croce
Via Magliabechi
Santa
Croce
Cappella
dei Pazzi
Largo
Piero Bargellini
Via S Giuseppe
Via de'
Via de' Malcontenti
Via de S Giuseppe
Vinegia
Palazzo dei
Da Diacceto
Borgo dei Neri
Museo
Horne
Corso d'Tintori
Biblioteca
Nazionale
SANTA CROCE
Piazza de'
Cavalleggeri
Torre delle
Zecca
Piazza
Piave
Via Tripoli
Diaz
VIA DEI BENCI
Lungarno Delle Grazie
Lungarno Della Zecca Vecchia
LUNGARNO
PECORI GIRALDI
PONTE ALLE
GRAZIE

G   H   J

Bargello

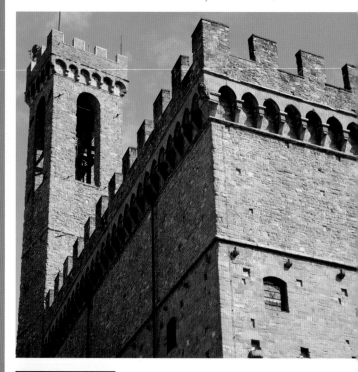

HIGHLIGHTS

- Donatello's *David*
- Giambologna's *Mercury*
- Giambologna's animals
- Michelangelo's *Bacchus*
- Della Robbia's terracottas
- Courtyard

TIPS

● The museum is very popular and in high season it is best to book in advance.
● When planning your visit, note that the museum closes at 2.

This superb medieval building, with its massive walls, vaulted rooms and airy courtyard, makes the perfect setting for one of the world's finest collections of Renaissance sculpture.

Diverse uses Built in 1255, the Bargello was the first seat of Florence's city government and served as the city's main law court before being passed to the Bargello (Chief of Police) in 1574; it was used as a prison until 1859. In 1865 it opened as a museum, focusing on Renaissance sculpture and decorative arts.

Courtyard art The courtyard walls, once the site of executions, carry the coats of arms of the *podestà* (chief magistrates), whose head-quarters were here, and 16th-century sculpture,

Clockwise from left: The Bargello's striking facade up close; the arcaded courtyard; statues line the vaulted walkways; Giambologna's Oceanus

including Giambologna's *Oceanus* from the Boboli Gardens. The ground floor has his *Mercury* (1564) and important works by Michelangelo and Cellini.

Sculpture, medals and bronzes The Salone del Consiglio Generale, a vaulted hall on the first floor, was once the courtroom. It has works by Donatello, including his bronze *David* (c. 1430–40), dressed in long boots and a jaunty hat, and his *St. George* (1416), sculpted for the exterior of Orsanmichele (▷ 39). On the second floor, enamel terracottas by the della Robbia family include the bust of a boy by Andrea della Robbia. Note the displays of Italian medals and small Renaissance bronzes. The arms room houses ivory-inlay saddles, guns and armour.

Cappella dei Pazzi

The serene cloisters of Cappella dei Pazzi

THE BASICS

santacroceopera.it
🔢 H6
✉ Piazza Santa Croce
☎ 055 246 6105
🕐 Mon–Sat 9.30–5,
Sun 2–5
🚌 C1, C2, C3
♿ Good
🎫 Moderate; joint ticket
with Santa Croce and
Museo dell'Opera
❓ Access is through
Santa Croce

HIGHLIGHTS

● Cloister
● Roundels of the evangelists
● Cimabue's crucifix (13th century)
● Taddeo Gaddi's fresco (1333)
● Donatello's *St. Louis of Toulouse* (1424)
● Museo dell'Opera

The balanced architecture of the quiet cloisters of Santa Croce, the approach to the Cappella dei Pazzi, embodies the rationality and harmony that are the keystones of the Renaissance artistic spirit.

Convent building On the south side of Santa Croce (▷ 33) are the buildings of a former convent. These include the Cappella dei Pazzi, one of the great architectural masterpieces of the early Renaissance, and a 14th-century refectory, which houses the Museo dell'Opera di Santa Croce. This is one of the lowest-lying areas in Florence, and to the left of the Cappella dei Pazzi a plaque almost 6m (20ft) up shows the high point of the November 1966 floodwaters. The second cloister, a haven of calm, was designed by Filippo Brunelleschi.

The Pazzi Chapel The Cappella, which was commissioned as a chapter house by Andrea dei Pazzi and designed by Brunelleschi (*c.*1430), is incorporated into the cloisters. This domed chapel is in *pietra serena* (grey sandstone) against a white plaster background, embellished only by terracotta roundels.

Small but beautiful The museum contains many important works, including a restored crucifix by Giovanni Cimabue. On the walls a huge fresco by Taddeo Gaddi shows the Last Supper and Mary Magdalene washing Christ's feet. Prominent is Donatello's gilded bronze statue of St. Louis of Toulouse (1424).

Museo Galileo

Museum facade (left); the astrolabe of Gualtiero Arsenio (right)

This fascinating museum, with its state-of-the-art themed exhibits, puts Florence firmly among the major players in the development of science. Pick up one of the excellent audio-visual guides to get the best from your visit.

Pure science Focusing on imaginatively displayed scientific and mathematical instruments, the museum traces the role played by Florence in the development of modern science. Its core collection, dating from 1775, was acquired largely by the Medici Grand Dukes and has been displayed in the 14th-century Palazzo Castellani since 1929.

The Medici and Galileo Galilei The role of the Medici, Florence's dynastic ruling family from the 14th to the 18th centuries, in scientific study is appraised via scientific instruments, and there is a fascinating section devoted to maps, globes and navigation. Look out in particular for the sumptuous armillary sphere, used to divine the movements of the planets, made for the Medici in 1590. Pisa-born scientist Galileo (1564–1642) gets star billing, with his telescopes and compasses on display—there is even a reliquary containing his finger bones.

Monumental sundial The giant sundial outside the museum was built in 2007 as a "mathematical ornament." Look for the lizard-viper on the bronze gnomon whose tail shadow indicates midday.

THE BASICS

museogalileo.it

🔳 F6

✉ Piazza dei Giudici 1

☎ 055 265 311

🕐 Wed–Mon 9.30–6, Tue 9.30–1

🚌 C3

♿ Excellent

💷 Expensive

❓ Excellent guide book

HIGHLIGHTS

- Galileo's telescope
- Lopo Homem's map of the world (16th century)
- Antonio Santucci's armillary sphere (1573)
- Copy of Lorenzo della Volpaia's clock of the planets (1593)
- Monumental sundial
- Gualtiero Arsenio's astrolabe

Galleria degli Uffizi

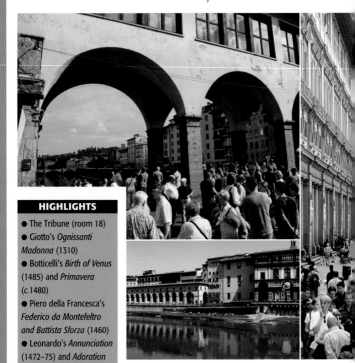

HIGHLIGHTS

● The Tribune (room 18)
● Giotto's *Ognissanti Madonna* (1310)
● Botticelli's *Birth of Venus* (1485) and *Primavera* (c.1480)
● Piero della Francesca's *Federico da Montefeltro and Battista Sforza* (1460)
● Leonardo's *Annunciation* (1472–75) and *Adoration of the Magi* (1481)
● Michelangelo's *Holy Family* (1508)
● Titian's *Venus of Urbino* (1538)

TIPS

● Reserve in advance; the wait can be up to 3 hours.
● Plan what you want to see as backtracking is difficult.
● Be patient as highlights are often blocked by groups.
● There are often long waits for the toilet, so go before you arrive.

The world-famous Uffizi encompasses the artistic developments of the Renaissance period and beyond. It is a powerful expression of Florence's extraordinary role in the history of art.

Medici art The gallery contains part of the Medici's art collection, bequeathed in 1737 by Anna Maria Luisa. The building was designed by Vasari, in the 1560s, as the administrative offices (*uffizi*) of the Grand Duchy.

It's all about paintings Today visitors flock to the Uffizi to admire the greatest collection of Renaissance painting in the world. It is displayed in chronological order and by school, starting with the first stirrings of the Renaissance in the 13th century and ending with works by

Clockwise from far left: The Corridoio Vasariano, linking the Uffizi with the Palazzo Pitti, crossing the Ponte Vecchio; crowds gather outside the Uffizi; detail of Filippo Lippi's *Madonna with Child and Two Angels;* the gallery seen from the River Arno

Caravaggio, Rembrandt and Canaletto from the 17th and 18th centuries. Uccello's *Battle of San Romano* (1456) exemplifies the technical advances of the Renaissance, while Filippo Lippi's *Madonna with Child and Two Angels* (c.1465) reveals the emotional focus typical of the period.

Venus Perhaps the most fascinating room is the Tribune, an octagonal chamber with a mother-of-pearl ceiling. In the middle is the Medici *Venus*, whose sensuous derrière earned her the reputation of the sexiest sculpture of the ancient world. Portraits include Bronzino's *Giovanni de Medici* (c.1549), a smiling boy holding a goldfinch. The café provides a welcome pitstop and has superb views of Piazza della Signoria.

THE BASICS

uffizi.it

F6

Loggiato degli Uffizi 6

055 238 8651
(reserve ahead to avoid queues by calling 055 294 883 or online at webshop b-ticket.com)

Tue–Sun 8.15–6.50 (last admission 45 min before closing)

Café

C1, C2

Good

Expensive

Palazzo Vecchio

TOP 25

From left: View from the top; Salone dei Cinquecento; the palace's striking facade

From left: View from the top; Salone dei Cinquecento; the palace's striking facade

THE BASICS

cultura.comune.fi.it

🔖 F6

✉ Piazza della Signoria

☎ 055 276 8224

🕒 Apr–Sep Fri–Wed 9am–11pm, Thu 9–2; Oct–Mar Fri–Wed 9–7, Thu 9–2

🚌 C1, C2

♿ Good

💶 Expensive

HIGHLIGHTS

- Sala delle Carte
- Sala dei Gigli
- Michelangelo's *Genius of Victory*
- Donatello's *Judith and Holofernes*
- View from the Terrazza di Saturno
- Salone dei Cinquecento

With its fortress-like castellations and its commanding 95m (311ft) bell tower, the Palazzo Vecchio conveys a message of political power supported by solid military strength.

Town hall The Palazzo Vecchio is still Florence's town hall, as it has been since its completion by Arnolfo di Cambio in 1302. Duke Cosimo I made it his palace in 1540, but it became known as the Palazzo Vecchio (Old Palace) when Cosimo transferred his court to the Palazzo Pitti. When Florence was briefly the capital of Italy (1865–70), the building housed the Parliament and Foreign Ministry.

Assembly room The vast Salone dei Cinquecento is 18m (59ft) high and was designed in the 1490s, during the era of the Florentine Republic, as the meeting place of the 500-strong ruling assembly. Vasari painted the military scenes of Florence's victory over Siena and Pisa (1563–65). The theme of Florence's might is underscored by Michelangelo's *Genius of Victory* (1533–34), as well as sculptures of the *Deeds of Hercules* by Vincenzo dei Rossi.

Loggia views On the second floor the Terrazza di Saturno is an open loggia with views to the hills. The Sala dei Gigli is decorated with gold fleurs-de-lys and houses Donatello's *Judith and Holofernes* (1456–60). The Sala delle Carte (Map Room), has a collection of maps painted on leather, showing the world in 1563.

Piazza della Signoria

From left: Neptune sculpture; statue of Duke Cosimo I; Palazzo de Leone

THE BASICS

🞦 F6
✉ Piazza della Signoria
🚌 C1, C2
♿ Good

HIGHLIGHTS

● Loggia dei Lanzi (1376)
● Cellini's *Perseus* (1554)
● Giambologna's *Rape of the Sabine Women* (1583)
● Ammannati's *Neptune* (1575)
● Rivoire café
● Sorbi newspaper and postcard kiosk

Standing in the Piazza della Signoria in the shadow of the towering Palazzo Vecchio, it is impossible to escape the sense of Florence's past political might.

Political piazza The Piazza della Signoria has been the hub of political life in Florence since the 14th century. It was the scene of great triumphs, such as the return of the Medici in 1530, but also of the Bonfire of the Vanities instigated by Savonarola, who was himself burned at the stake here in 1498, denounced as a heretic by the Inquisition.

Significant sculptures The sculptures here bristle with political connotations, many of them fiercely contradictory. Michelangelo's *David* (the original is in the Accademia) was placed outside the Palazzo Vecchio as a symbol of the Republic's defiance of the Medici. The *Neptune* (1575), by Ammannati, celebrates Medici maritime ambitions, and Giambologna's statue of Duke Cosimo I (1595) the man who brought all of Tuscany under Medici rule. The statue of Perseus holding Medusa's head (1554), by Cellini, is a stark reminder of what happened to those who crossed the Medici. The graceful Loggia dei Lanzi, now an open-air sculpture gallery, was designed by Orcagna in 1376.

Postcard paradise Sorbi, the newspaper kiosk, has a superb collection of postcards and newspapers, which you could enjoy over a drink in the Rivoire café (▷ 50).

Santa Croce

Santa Croce's distinctive marble exterior houses many treasures

Santa Croce, the largest Franciscan church in Italy, combines architectural and artistic treasures on a grand scale with a very human atmosphere.

Burial place Santa Croce, rebuilt for the Franciscan order in 1294 by Arnolfo di Cambio, is the burial place of the great and the good in Florence. Michelangelo is buried in Santa Croce, as are Rossini, Machiavelli and the Pisa-born Galileo Galilei, who was excommunicated during the Inquisition and was not allowed a Christian burial until 1737, 95 years after his death. There is also a memorial to Dante, whose sarcophagus is empty.

Anglophile The exterior is covered with a poly-chrome marble facade added in 1863 and paid for by the English benefactor Sir Francis Sloane. It overlooks the Piazza Santa Croce, site of an annual football game in medieval costume.

Artistic riches The artistic wealth in Santa Croce is stunning; frescoes by Gaddi (1380) in the Cappella Maggiore tell the story of the holy cross ("Santa Croce"), and beautiful frescoes by Giotto in the Bardi and Peruzzi chapels show scenes from the lives of St. Francis and St. John the Evangelist. The memorial to 19th-century playwright Giovanni Battista Nicolini, left of the entrance facing the altar, is said to have inspired the *Statue of Liberty*. Santa Croce was severely hit by flooding in 1966, and you can still see a tide mark showing far up on the pillars and walls.

THE BASICS

santacroceopera.it
✚ H6
✉ Piazza Santa Croce
☎ 055 246 6105
🕐 Mon–Sat 9.30–5, Sun 2–5; closed during services
🚍 C1, C2, C3
♿ Good
✋ Expensive

HIGHLIGHTS

● Giotto's frescoes (1320–25)
● Tombs of Michelangelo, Machiavelli and Galileo
● Painted wooden ceiling
● Donatello's *Annunciation* (1435)
● Polychrome marble facade (1863)
● Wooden crucifix by Donatello
● 14th-century windows
● Cappella dei Pazzi (▷ 26)

Ponte Vecchio

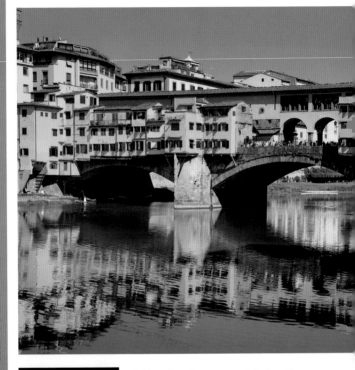

HIGHLIGHTS

- Gold and jewellery shops
- Views of the Arno
- Corridoio Vasariano (1565)
- Bust of Cellini (1900)

TIP

- The sun sets directly downriver from the bridge, and the golden tones of the structure itself are magical on a good evening.

Linking the city centre with the Oltrarno for over 700 years, the bustling Ponte Vecchio, as much a street as a bridge, is lined with jewellers and goldsmiths, their shops jutting precariously over the river.

The test of time Near the Roman crossing, the Old Bridge was, until 1218, the only bridge across the Arno in Florence. The current bridge dates from 1345. During World War II, it was the only bridge the Germans did not destroy, though they did demolish the buildings either side. The bridge's luck held again in 1966, when it survived the November flood.

Private path When the Medici moved from the Palazzo Vecchio to the Palazzo Pitti, they decided they needed a connecting route from

Clockwise from left: Ponte Vecchio seen from Ponte Santa Trinita; bust of the sculptor, soldier and goldsmith Benvenuto Cellini guarding the bridge; the Corridoio Vasariano, running along Lungarno Archibusieri, connects the Uffizi to Ponte Vecchio and the Oltrarno

the Uffizi to the Palazzo Pitti on the other side of the river that enabled them to keep out of contact with their people. The result was Vasari's Corridoio Vasariano, built in 1565 above Lungarno Archibusieri and on top of the buildings lining the bridge's eastern parapet.

Glitz Shops have been on the Ponte Vecchio since the 13th century. Initially there were all types—butchers and fishmongers and later tanners, whose industrial waste caused a pretty rank stench. In 1593 Medici Duke Ferdinand I decreed that only goldsmiths and jewellers be allowed on the bridge. As it is a prime tourist destination and one of the places that Florentines regularly come to for the *passeggiata*, it is also always packed and attracts street vendors, hawking fake goods.

Via de' Tornabuoni

TOP 25

History meets style on the smartest street in town

THE BASICS

- ⊞ E5–E6
- ✉ Via de' Tornabuoni
- 🚌 C2
- ♿ Good

HIGHLIGHTS

- Sassetti Chapel frescoes in Santa Trinita
- Ferragamo shoe museum
- Designer shops
- Palazzo Strozzi
- 17th-century facade of San Gaetano

Florence may be one of the world's richest cultural cities, but it's also a place for serious shopping. Fashionable Via de' Tornabuoni supports the top names in fashion, with chic boutiques vying for space with grand palaces.

Shopping in palaces Italy has always been synonymous with style—think Milan or Rome—but Florence contributes in its own way, too. The city hosted Italy's earliest fashion shows in the 1950s, and innovative designers made their fortunes within the city's medieval palaces here on Via de' Tornabuoni. Salvatore Ferragamo, the flagship store and shoe museum (▷ 38), can be found within the Palazzo Spini Feroni, one of the best-preserved private medieval palaces in Florence; while Guccio Gucci picked this street—three generations ago—for his head-quarters, which is still based at 73r Tornabuoni. As you browse, spare a moment to glance up at the facades of the imposing buildings.

Beyond the shops At the north end of the street is the stunning Palazzo Antinori (1465), next to the city's greatest baroque church, San Gaetano (1648), a tranquil spot to escape the crowds. At the south end is Piazza Santa Trinita, with its artistically rich church. Central to the square is the tall Column of Justice, brought from the Baths of Caracalla in Rome and given to Cosimo I in 1560 by Pope Pius IV. Just beyond here is the Santa Trinita Bridge (▷ 39), which links elegant Tornabuoni with Oltrarno.

More to See

BADIA FIORENTINA
The Badia Fiorentina, the oldest monastery in Florence, was founded in AD978 by Willa, widow of Umberto, Margrave of Tuscany. It is best known for its connection with the medieval poet Dante, who used to meet Beatrice here. Its magnificent bell tower is Gothic at the top and Romanesque at the base. Inside are two notable works: Filippino Lippi's *The Madonna Appearing to St. Bernard*, left of the entrance, and the tomb of Count Ugo, son of Willa and Umberto, in the left transept.

🔠 G6 ✉ Via del Proconsolo ☎ 055 264 402 🕐 Mon 3–6 🚇 C2 ♿ Impossible 🎫 Free

CASA BUONARROTI
casabuonarroti.it
This house, which Michelangelo bought in 1508, is now a fascinating museum and gallery. Exhibits include the artist's earliest known work, the *Madonna della Scala* (*c.*1491), a wood and wax model

(the only one of its type) of a river god, and a model of the facade for San Lorenzo never executed.

🔠 H6 ✉ Via Ghibellina 70 ☎ 055 241 698 🚇 C2 🕐 Mar–Oct Wed–Mon 10–5; Nov–Feb Wed–Mon 10–4. Guided tours can be reserved ♿ Poor 🎫 Moderate

CASA DI DANTE
museocasadidante.it
The 13th-century House of Dante contains material relating to the author's life and work.

🔠 F6 ✉ Via Santa Margherita 1 ☎ 055 219 416 🕐 Apr–Sep daily 10–6; Oct–Mar Tue–Sun 10–5 🚇 C1, C2 ♿ None 🎫 Inexpensive

MERCATO NUOVO
So-called to distinguish it from the Mercato Vecchio, which closed in the 16th century, this market is famous for the brass boar with a well-stroked nose, *Il Porcellino*.

🔠 F6 ✉ Loggiato del Porcellino, Via Porta Rossa 🕐 Mid-Mar to Oct daily 9–8; Nov to mid-Mar Tue–Sun 9–7.30 🚇 C1, C2 ♿ Good (but crowded)

Casa di Dante

Mercato Nuovo

MERCATO SANT'AMBROGIO

mercatosantambrogio.it

After the Mercato Centrale, this is the second most important market for fresh produce in Florence. It is inexpensive and pleasantly noisy.

H6 ☒ Piazza Lorenzo Ghiberti ⊙ Mon–Sat 7–2 🚌 C2, C3 ♿ Good

MUSEO HORNE

museohorne.it

This small museum, housed in Palazzo Corsi, owes its existence to English art historian and collector Herbert Percy Horne (1864– 1916). Horne bought the palazzo in 1904 for his collection of paintings, furniture and sculpture, and left both to Italy on his death.

G7 ☒ Via de Benci 6 ☎ 055 244 661 ⊙ Thu–Tue 10–4 🚌 23, B, C ♿ None 🎫 Moderate

MUSEO SALVATORE FERRAGAMO

ferragamo.com

Founded in 1995, this collection of 10,000 pairs of shoes by Ferragamo dates from his return from Hollywood to Florence in 1927. The collection highlights Ferragamo's choice of colours, his imaginative models and experimentation with materials. Many pairs were created for celebrities such as Ava Gardner, Judy Garland and Marilyn Monroe.

E6 ☒ Palazzo Spini Feroni, Piazza Santa Trinita 5r ☎ 055 356 2417 ⊙ Daily 10–7.30 🚌 C3, 6 ♿ Poor 🎫 Moderate

OGNISSANTI

This was the parish church of both the Vespucci family and Botticelli; he was buried here. In the second chapel on the right, facing the altar, is a fresco by Ghirlandaio, which is said to include Amerigo Vespucci's portrait (the boy behind the Virgin). Ghirlandaio's painting of St. Jerome is also here, opposite Botticelli's St. Augustine in his study. The real star is in the convent's *cenacolo* (refectory), where the back wall is covered by Ghirlandaio's magnificent *Last Supper* fresco.

Magnificent frescoes adorn the ceiling and walls of the Ognissanti

➕ D5 ✉ Borgo Ognissanti 42 ☎ 055 239 8700 🕐 Daily 7–12.30, 4–8. *Last Supper* in convent Mon, Tue, Sat 9–12 🚌 C3, D ♿ Poor 🎫 Free

ORSANMICHELE

Built as a grain market in 1337, Orsanmichele became a church in 1380. The city's guilds commissioned some of the best artists to make statues of patron saints to sit in the canopied niches, and so created a permanent exhibition of 15th-century Florentine sculpture. These statues have now all been removed and replaced by copies; the originals are in the Bargello or Orsanmichele museums.

➕ F6 ✉ Via dei Calzaiuoli ☎ 055 284 944 🕐 Daily 10–5 🚌 C1 ♿ Good 🎫 Free

PIAZZA DELLA REPUBBLICA

This grandiose square on the site of the Roman forum dates from the 1870s, after Florence was briefly the capital of Italy. Florentines are not fond of the square's architecture nor its crass neoclassical triumphal arch, but it is a fine open space where you can breathe a little. It's lined with grand cafés and touristy restaurants.

➕ F6 🚌 C2 ♿ Good

PONTE SANTA TRÌNITA

The finest of Florence's bridges dates back to 1252, although what you see today is a well-executed replica of Ammannati's version, built in 1567 and destroyed by the Nazis in 1944. Ammannati was commissioned by Cosimo I and probably consulted Michelangelo in his designs. Lovely views of Florence, especially the Ponte Vecchio, are to be had from here.

➕ E6 🚌 C3, D ♿ Good 🎫 Free

SAN MARTINO DEL VESCOVO

This tiny oratory is set right in the heart of medieval Florence. Don't miss the *lunette* frescoes on the upper walls.

➕ F6 ✉ Piazza San Martino, Via Dante Alighieri 🕐 Mon–Sat 10–12, 3–5 (closed Fri pm) 🚌 C2 ♿ Acceptable 🎫 Free

Ponte Santa Trinita

Piazza della Repubblica

Dante's Florence

A short walk through the district where Dante lived, worked and played, and then on to the eastern part of the city to Sante Croce.

DISTANCE: 1km (0.5 miles) approx **ALLOW:** 1.5 hours including visits

START

BATTISTERO (▷ 54–55)
🟦 F5 🚌 C1, C2

END

SANTA CROCE (▷ 33)
🟦 H6 🚌 C1, C2, C3

❶ Start at the Baptistery (▷ 54–55), where the poet Dante Alighieri was baptized. At that time, it was not covered with the marble facing that adorns the facade today.

❷ According to tradition, Dante watched the construction of the cathedral from the Sasso di Dante, a stone (marked) in the wall between Via dello Studio and Via del Proconsolo, opposite the Duomo.

❸ Take Via dello Studio. Turn left at Via del Corso and take the first right onto Via di Santa Margherita. This leads to the Casa di Dante (▷ 37), one-time home of the author.

❹ Opposite is San Martino del Vescovo (▷ 39), where Dante's family worshipped. Back towards Via del Corso is Santa Margherita, where his Beatrice went to Mass.

❺ From Santa Margherita turn left onto Via Dante Alighieri for the entrance of the Badia (▷ 37).

❻ Dante often saw Beatrice here and the Badia's bell would have punctuated Dante's daily life. Exit and turn onto Via del Proconsolo, past the Bargello (▷ 24–25), which was being built in Dante's time.

❼ Take the second left, Via dell'Anguillara, to reach Piazza Santa Croce. The streets are dotted with artisans' workshops. Outside the church of Santa Croce (▷ 33) there is a 19th-century statue of Dante.

❽ Dante's sarcophagus, inside the church, is empty. Despite all his connections with the city of Florence, Dante was buried in Ravenna.

Shopping

ANGELA CAPUTI

angelacaputi.com

Angela Caputi is the place to look for bright, bold and highly original costume jewellery, all of which is handmade in Oltrarno. Clothing and accessories to go with the pendant or earrings you have just bought are also stocked. There is another branch at Via Santo Spirito 58r.

🔲 F6 ✉ Borgo Santi Apostoli 44–46r ☎ 055 292 993 🚌 C3, D

ANICHINI

anichini.net

The 15th-century Palazzo Ricasoli is the setting for this shop, selling exquisite children's clothing up to age 14 years. Traditional christening robes are trimmed with lace, while for older children there are frilly, smocked frocks, coats and smart suits.

🔲 E6 ✉ Via del Parione 59r ☎ 055 284 977 🚌 C3, D

AQUAFLOR

florenceparfum.it

Master perfumer Sileno Cheloni's shop is located within the vaulted rooms of a Renaissance palazzo. The bespoke perfumes, colognes, soaps, creams, lotions and candles—all produced on site—make wonderful gifts. Try the tomato leaf hand cream.

🔲 G6 ✉ Via Borgo Santa Croce 6r ☎ 346 724 3083 🚌 C1, C3

ARMANDO POGGI

apoggi.com

This famous shop stocks one of the widest selections of porcelain in the city, including Giuseppe Armani figurines and Richard Ginori pieces, as well as silverware and Murano glass.

🔲 F5 ✉ Via Calzaiuoli 103r ☎ 055 211 719 🚌 C2

BACCANI

giovannibaccani.it

This beautiful old shop, established in 1903, stocks handmade picture frames, prints, engravings and old maps. Prices vary from very reasonable to very expensive.

🔲 D5 ✉ Borgo Ognissanti 22r ☎ 055 214 467 🚌 C3

BENHEART

benheart.it

For that really special leather item, head to this idiosyncratic store, where you'll find one-off slouchy bags, cutting-edge leather jackets, quirky ankle boots and moccasins and all kinds of leather accessories. Items can be customized or bespoke and shipped anywhere in the world.

🔲 E6 ✉ Via della Vigna Nuova 97r ☎ 055 239 9483 🚌 C2

IL BISONTE

ilbisonte.com

All items sold by this cutting-edge leatherware brand come stamped with the trademark bison.

🔲 E6 ✉ Via del Parione 31r ☎ 055 215 722 🚌 C3

GOLD FACTS

A dazzling array of gold is for sale all over Florence, most notably on the Ponte Vecchio. In 1593 Ferdinand I decreed that only goldsmiths and jewellers should work there and it has remained that way ever since. The gold sold in Florence is 18 carat, often expressed as a rather confusing 750 per cent (with the per cent sign actually referring to 1,000). Gold is also found—at somewhat lower prices—in the Santa Croce area, where, in accordance with tradition, all gold jewellery is sold by weight.

CASSETTI

cassetti.it

Maria Grazia's collection of jewellery, including period items, has caught the eye of famous people over the years, including David Bowie and Liz Taylor.

🏠 F6 ✉ Ponte Vecchio 33–52–54r ☎ 055 287 361 🚌 C3, D

CELLERINI

cellerini.it

Cellerini offers handmade elegant and sophisticated leather bags of outstanding quality. Styles tend to be wonderfully simple yet cleverly designed.

🏠 E5 ✉ Via del Sole 9 ☎ 055 282 533 🚌 C2, C3, D

COIN

coin.it

This department store stocks a wide range of men's and women's clothing, accessories, homewares and cosmetics—all at reasonable prices. The rooftop café has 360-degree views of the city.

🏠 F5 ✉ Via dei Calzaiuoli 56r ☎ 055 280 531 🚌 C2

EMILIO CAVALLINI

emiliocavallini.com

This wacky collection of socks and hosiery is a great source of gifts. Look out for boldly patterned black and white "mantyhose" and "meggings" for the more daring male.

🏠 E6 ✉ Via della Vigna Nuova 24r ☎ 055 238 2789 🚌 C3

EMILIO PUCCI

emiliopucci.com

This renowned Florentine fashion house was created in 1950 by Marquis Emilio Pucci. The boutique sells his trademark colourful silk shirts, separates, shoes and accessories. Prices are high!

🏠 E6 ✉ Via de' Tornabuoni 20–22r ☎ 055 265 8082 🚌 C3

FELTRINELLI

lafeltrinelli.it

Mega bookstore Feltrinelli is particularly strong on art and photography and has an excellent section of titles in English. The café is a good place for a coffee or light meal, and stays open until 11pm.

🏠 F5 ✉ Piazza della Repubblica 26–29 ☎ 02 9194 7777 🚌 C2

FLORENCE FACTORY

florencefactory.it

This imaginative outlet showcases the best of contemporary Florentine and Tuscan workmanship with a modern twist. They sell artisan-produced homewares and fashion and accessories, with the accent on new design talent.

🏠 G6 ✉ Via dei Neri 6/8r ☎ 055 205 2952 🚌 C2

FRATELLI PICCINI

fratellipiccini.com

If you go jewellery shopping on the Ponte Vecchio, make sure you include Piccini's. They have lovely gold charms, which make a nice gift.

🏠 F6 ✉ Ponte Vecchio 23r ☎ 055 294 768 🚌 C3, D

STYLISH CITY

One of Florence's many claims to fame is as the headquarters of Gucci. It was also in Florence, in 1927, that Salvatore Ferragamo established himself, after having made his reputation in Hollywood crafting shoes for the likes of Greta Garbo, Vivien Leigh and the gladiators in Cecil B. de Mille costume epics. This family still administers a fashion empire, producing accessories and clothes as well as the trademark shoes.

FURLA

furla.com

Furla produces chic leather bags and belts at prices that are less astronomical than elsewhere.

➕ F5 ✉ Via Calzaiuoli 10r ☎ 055 238 2883 🖥 C2

LEATHER SCHOOL OF SANTA CROCE

scuoladelcuoio.com

At the back of Santa Croce church, this workshop sells quality hand-crafted bags, wallets and accessories at the on-site shop.

➕ G6 ✉ Via San Guiseppe 5r (off Piazza Santa Croce) ☎ 055 244 533 🖥 C1, C2, C3

LETIZIA FIORINI

This beautiful little shop is also the artist's workshop, where she makes charming, and not expensive, hand-crafted puppets, dolls and other toys. It's hard to resist buying a Pinocchio puppet or a jack-in-the-box to take home.

➕ E6 ✉ Via del Parione 60r ☎ 055 216 504 🖥 C3

LUISA VIA ROMA

luisaviaroma.com

A popular spot for Florence's image-conscious men and women, Luisa's famous, eye-catching window displays conceal a sleek interior over two floors where well-known labels rub shoulders with in-house designs.

➕ F5 ✉ Via Roma 19–21r ☎ 055 906 4116 🖥 C2

MARTELLI

martelligloves.it

This Florence institution has hand made gloves since 1967 and sells an amazing selection, in every hue and fabric imaginable.

WHAT'S AN ANTIQUE

Under Italian law an antique need not be old, but need only be made of old materials. For this reason, what would be called reproduction elsewhere is called an antique in Italy. Many shops in Florence sell antiques, from the glamorous international emporia on Borgo Ognissanti to the flea market in Piazza dei Ciompi—there are whole streets of them. The most important include Borgo Ognissanti and Via Maggio, for very expensive antiques finely displayed.

➕ F6 ✉ Via Por Santa Maria 18r ☎ 055 239 6395 🖥 C3, D

MISURI

leatherguild.it

Housed in frescoed Palazzo Antellesi, this is one of the oldest leather factories and shops in Santa Croce. Misuri produces top-quality jackets, handbags and briefcases, wallets, shoes and small accessories such as leather bookmarks. It is correspondingly pricey.

➕ G6 ✉ Piazza Santa Croce 20r ☎ 055 240 995 🖥 C1, C2, C3

OFFICINA PROFUMO-FARMACEUTICA DI SANTA MARIA NOVELLA

smnovella.it

Housed in a 13th-century frescoed chapel, this beautiful pharmacy sells lotions and potions, soaps, candles, perfumes and herbal remedies, still made to recipes handed down from Dominican friars. Many of the products have an interesting history, such as the perfume commissioned by Catherine de Medici for her wedding in 1533.

➕ D5 ✉ Via della Scala 16 ☎ 055 216 276 🖥 C2, D

OLFATTORIO

olfattorio.it

Even if you don't want to buy, take a look at the striking display and interior of this perfumery. Let an expert find the fragrance to suit you, most of which are handmade in France or the UK. There is also a quirky little museum dedicated to early 20th-century powder boxes.

⊞ E6 ⊠ Via de' Tornabuoni 6 ☎ 055 286 925 🚇 C3

OTISOPSE

otisopse.com

Otisopse sells classic leather footwear for men and women at bargain prices and in a fantastic range of colours; you'll find everything from soft suede moccasins and ballerina pumps to classic brogues and Chelsea boots.

⊞ F6 ⊠ Via Porta Rossa 13r ☎ 081 1817 2718 🚇 C3, D

PAMPALONI

pampaloni.com

This shop is known for its high-quality sterling silver and silver-plated tableware, gifts and accessories, and its gleaming window displays are often eye-catching and provocative.

⊞ F6 ⊠ Via Porta Rossi 99r ☎ 055 289 094 🚇 C3, D

PARENTI

parentifirenze.it

Florentines come to this well-established store to stock up on home accessories, lamps, crystal, tableware and porcelain, as well as jewellery. The range is huge—you can buy everything from a solid silver tray to a frog-shaped plant holder, and the store has the top international brands as well.

⊞ E6 ⊠ Via de' Tornabuoni 93r ☎ 055 214 438 🚇 C3

PARIONE

parione.it

This prestigious printing workshop sells hand-decorated marbled paper, customized stationery and accessories; the personalized pencils or Florentine papers make good take-home gifts.

⊞ F5 ⊠ Via dello Studio 11r ☎ 055 215 030 🚇 C1

PEGNA

pegna.it

This lovely old-fashioned shop, around since 1860, sells its delicious foods supermarket-style. Buy fine cheeses, olive oils, cakes, wines, salamis, chocolates and lots more.

⊞ F5 ⊠ Via dello Studio 8 ☎ 055 282 701/2 🚇 C2

PINEIDER

pineider.com

Pineider's exclusive stationery and book-binding business was founded in 1774. One of the characteristic papers covering diaries and address books is decorated with great artists' signatures. It is also known for its fountain pen range.

⊞ F6 ⊠ Piazza Rucellai 6r ☎ 055 284 656 🚇 C3

LA RINASCENTE
rinascente.it

This classy department store is stuffed with designer labels for both men and women at good prices. You'll also find perfumery, lingerie and homewares, and gourmet delicacies from all over Italy in the fourth-floor food market. The wonderful rooftop café has a terrace and offers magnificent views.

➕ F5 ✉ Piazza della Repubblica 1 ☎ 02 9138 7388 🚇 C2

SALVATORE FERRAGAMO
salvatoreferragamo.it

Considered to be *the* leading brand in Italian shoes and bags, Salvatore Ferragamo's unique collection is sold in his boutique in Palazzo Spini-Feroni, where the poor boy from Naples set up shop in 1927. When you've finished shopping, you can visit the shoe museum around the corner (▷ 38).

➕ E6 ✉ Via de' Tornabuoni 4r–14r ☎ 055 292 123 🚇 C2

VALMAR
This compact shop sells trims and finishings for fashion and upholstery.

➕ F6 ✉ Via Porta Rossa 53r ☎ 055 284 493 🚇 C1, C2, C3

VANDA NENCIONI
This is the place to come for pretty gilded frames, as well as period and modern prints.

➕ H6 ✉ Via dei Macci 27r ☎ 055 215 345 🚇 C2, C3

Entertainment and Nightlife

CHIESA DI SANTO STEFANO AL PONTE
classictic.com

The deconsecrated 11th-century church of Santo Stefano has been converted into an auditorium used for concerts and the occasional theatrical production.

➕ F6 ✉ Piazza di Santo Stefano 5 ☎ 055 217 418 🚇 C3, D

COLLE BERETO
cafecollebereto.com

Colle Bereto has a sophisticated vibe and a chic clientele who come for pre-dinner cocktails and nibbles. The terrace is a popular spot on sultry summer nights.

➕ F6 ✉ Piazza Strozzi 5r ☎ 055 283 156 🚇 C2

HARRY'S BAR
harrysbarfirenze.it

This American bar, on the banks of the Arno, is a great place for cocktails and has seen its share of celebrity visitors. The international food is also good.

➕ D6 ✉ Lungarno Vespucci 22r ☎ 055 239 6700 🚇 C3, D

MOYO
moyo.it

This buzzy Santa Croce bar has an outdoor terrace and a moody, high-tech interior that fills up at aperitivo time. DJ sets kick in later and it closes at 3am. It's popular during the day too.

➕ G6 ✉ Via de' Benci 23r ☎ 055 247 9738 🚇 C1, C3, D

LE MURATE

lemurate.it

Built as a convent, and later a prison, this space has been restored to provide a tantalizing multicultural venue. There's an art bar, literary events and food and drink throughout the day, but most people come here after 9.30 for the rock bands and DJs.

🔲 J6 ⊠ Piazza delle Murate 1 ☎ 055 234 6872 🚍 C2, C3

EVENING STROLL

Going out in Florence in the evening doesn't have to mean actually going anywhere. In summer a really enjoyable and popular way of spending time after dinner is to stroll through the streets of the *centro storico*, stopping off for an ice cream or a drink at a bar. You'll be in good company: Italians of all ages and genders will be doing exactly the same thing.

ODEON CINEHALL

odeonfirenze.it

Housed in the art nouveau Palazzo Strozzino, the cinema has original sculptures, tapestries and a stained-glass cupola. This is the best place in the city for undubbed films in English.

🔲 E6 ⊠ Piazza Strozzi ☎ 055 214 068 🕒 Times vary. Check the website for schedule 🚍 C2

TEATRO VERDI

teatroverdionline.it

The Teatro Verdi, founded in 1854, became the home of the excellent Orchestra della Toscana, which plays here between December and May. The theatre also stages drama, ballet, opera and pop and rock concerts.

🔲 G6 ⊠ Via Ghibellina 99 ☎ 055 212 320 🚍 14, 23, C2

Where to Eat

PRICES

Prices are approximate, based on a 3-course meal for one person.

€€€   over €60
€€   €40–€60
€   under €40

13 GOBBI (€€)

casatrattoria.com

Gobbi, with its candlelight and warm atmosphere, provides a romantic setting in which to enjoy traditional Tuscan fare with a lighter touch and tasty desserts.

🔲 D5 ⊠ Via del Porcellana 9r 🕒 Daily 12.30–3, 7.30–11 ☎ 055 284 015 🚍 C2

ARA: È SUD (€€€)

araristorante.it

If the meat-heavy Tuscan diet begins to pall, head to this temple of Sicilian gastronomy, where you'll find all the classic Sicilian dishes. There's always fresh fish on offer and genuine *cannoli* (fried dough with creamy filling) for dessert, accompanied by excellent Sicilian wines.

🔲 G6 ⊠ Via della Vogna Vecchia 4r ☎ 331 217 0926 🕒 Wed–Mon noon–11 🚍 C1, C2

BALDOVINO (€€)

baldovinobistrot.com

This bustling trattoria not far from Piazza Santa Croce serves great pizza, cooked

in a wood-burning oven, in a relaxed setting. The menu ranges from pizzas to salads to *bistecca alla Fiorentina*.
🔲 H6 ⊠ Via San Giuseppe 22r ☎ 055 241 773 🕙 Daily 11–11 🚇 C1, C2, C3

BELLE DONNE (€–€€)
belledonneosteria.com
An inexpensive option in an expensive part of town, this modest place offers traditional meat dishes as well as tasty vegetarian options such as *melanzane alla parmigiana* (aubergine and parmesan bake). You may well end up sharing your table with other customers.
🔲 E5 ⊠ Via delle Belle Donne 16r ☎ 055 238 2609 🕙 Daily noon–2.30, 7–11 🚇 C2

BOCCADAMA (€€)
Interesting food and good wine, plus views of the Basilica Santa Croce, make this lively historic *enoteca* popular. You can eat outside on the delightful terrace.
🔲 G6 ⊠ Piazza Santa Croce 25–26r ☎ 055 243 640 🕙 Daily 11–3, 6.30–10.30 🚇 C1, C2, C3

LA BUSSOLA (€€)
labussolafirenze.it
La Bussola serves some of the best pizza in town, cooked in a traditional wood-burning oven, plus good seafood dishes. The setting is rustic, the service relaxed, and you can eat perched up at the bar.
🔲 F6 ⊠ Via Porta Rossa 58r ☎ 055 293 376 🕙 Daily noon–10.30 🚇 C2, C3, D

CAFFÈ AMERINI (€)
Amerini lies in the main designer shopping area and gets very popular in the early afternoon. It serves sandwiches with tasty fillings and good pastries as well as light lunches.
🔲 E6 ⊠ Via della Vigna Nuova 63r ☎ 055 284 941 🕙 Daily 9–8 🚇 C2

CANTINETTA DEI VERRAZZANO (€€)
verrazzano.com
A wonderful wine bar-cum-shop selling breads baked on the premises, this place showcases wines from the Castello di Verrazzano estates near Greve. Don't miss the savoury focaccia baked in the wood-burning ovens.
🔲 F6 ⊠ Via dei Tavolini 18–20r ☎ 055 268 590 🕙 Mon–Sat 8am–9pm, Sun 10–4.30 🚇 C2

LA CARRAIA (€)
lacarraiagroup.eu
You'll find a huge range of ice-cream flavours and frozen desserts at this bright and friendly spot—choose from one of the classics, a seasonal fruit, or something different such as peanut butter, cookies and lemon cream or tiramisu.
🔲 H6 ⊠ Via dei Benci 24r ☎ 329 363 0069 🕙 Daily 11–9 🚇 C1, C2, C3

IL CIBRÈO (€€€)
cibreo.com
This restaurant, one of the city's gastronomic shrines, offers no pasta, but an intriguing range of robust Florentine dishes that vary with the seasons.

➕ H6 ✉ Via del Verrocchio 8r ☎ 055 234 1100 🕐 Tue–Sun 12.50–2.30, 6.50–11.15. Closed Aug 🚇 C2

COCO LEZZONE (€€€)

cocolezzone.it

Popular with Florentines, this place with informal white-tiled rooms offers Tuscan classics such as bread- and bean-based *ribollita* and rosemary-spiked *arista al forno* (roast pork).

➕ E6 ✉ Via del Parioncino 26r ☎ 055 287 178 🕐 Mon–Sat noon–2.15, 7–10.15. Closed Tue dinner 🚇 C3

DE' BENCI (€)

osteriadebenci.com

At this Florentine osteria you can start your meal with *crostini* (toasted bread served with liver pate), cheeses and cold meats, then choose from the day's menu, which often includes spaghetti in red wine and delicious vegetable soup. The meat dishes are particularly good.

➕ G6 ✉ Borgo Santa Croce 31r ☎ 055 234 4923 🕐 Mon–Thu 7.30pm–11pm, Fri–Sun 12.30–3, 7.30–11. Closed Aug 🚇 C1, C3

DEI FRESCOBALDI RISTORANTE & WINE BAR (€€)

frescobaldifirenze.it

On the corner of Piazza della Signoria, Frescobaldi offers traditional Tuscan cuisine, or the chance to eat tapas-style in the adjacent wine bar. In the main restaurant choose from pasta dishes or substantial grilled meats, complemented by an excellent wine list.

➕ F6 ✉ Via de' Magazzini 2–4r ☎ 055 284 724 🕐 Apr–Oct daily noon–midnight; Nov–Mar daily 12–3, 6.30–12 🚇 C3

DEL FAGIOLI (€)

A reliable place to sample authentic Florentine home cooking at reasonable

prices, wood-panelled Del Fagioli turns out delicious standards such as *ribollita* (bread and bean soup) and *bistecca* (Tuscan steak grilled over wood). Credit cards are not accepted.

➕ G7 ✉ Corso de' Tintori 47r ☎ 055 244 285 🕐 Mon–Fri 12.30–2.30, 7.30–10.30 🚇 C3, D

DIM SUM (€)

dimsumrestaurant.it

A refreshing change after all that rustic Florentine food, this contemporary dim sum restaurant serves delicious steamed dumplings and also makes its own noodles (in view of the diners). Lunch is a particular bargain.

➕ G6 ✉ Via Magliabechi 9r ☎ 055 284 331 🕐 Tue–Sun noon–3, 7–11 🚇 C1, C3, D

ENOTECA PINCHIORRI (€€€)

enotecapinchiorri.it

Set in a Renaissance palazzo with a delightful courtyard, this celebrated temple to Italian cuisine is one of only a handful of three-Michelin-starred restaurants in Italy. The ambience is elegant, the creative food superb, the wine list second to none and the service exquisite. Prices are very steep.

➕ G6 ✉ Via Ghibellina 87 ☎ 055 26311 🕐 Tue–Sat 7.30–10pm 🚇 C1, C2, C3

GILLI (€€)

caffegilli.it

This chic, opulent café in belle epoque style stands on the corner of the Piazza della Repubblica. Stand at the bar for a coffee and excellent pastry, or have a leisurely lunch on the terrace, where you can watch the world go by but prices are much higher.

➕ F5 ✉ Piazza della Repubblica 39r ☎ 055 213 896 ⏰ Daily 7.30am–1am 🚌 C2

GIUBBE ROSSE (€€)

giubberosse.it

This literary café was once the haunt of the Florentine avant-garde, and the red-jacketed waiters (that give the place its name) and stylish interiors hint at this illustrious past. Drink coffee and watch life on the piazza.

➕ F5 ✉ Piazza della Repubblica 13–14r ☎ 055 212 280 ⏰ Daily 10am–midnight 🚌 C2

KOME (€€)

komefirenze.it

This popular sushi and BBQ restaurant is housed in a historic palazzo under a gold-leaf ceiling. High stools stand alongside a winding counter; whether you sit here or at a table, the tempting sushi train will pass by you. Upstairs you grill your own meat and vegetables at your table.

> **PIZZA AT ITS BEST**
>
> As in every Italian town, pizzas are ubiquitous. Many shops sell *pizza a taglio* (pizza by the slice), which is a good option for a quick and inexpensive snack. In addition to the standard margherita pizza (tomato, mozzarella and basil), you will find all kinds of other delicious toppings, such as zucchini flowers and artichokes.

➕ G6 ✉ Via de' Benci 41r ☎ 055 200 8009 ⏰ Daily noon–3, 7.30–11 (sushi till midnight) 🚌 C1, C3

IL LATINI (€€)

illatini.com

This lively, informal restaurant, where you are likely to share a communal table, offers Tuscan classics such as *zuppa di fagioli* (bean soup) and one of the biggest T-bone steaks you'll ever see. Meat is a speciality.

➕ E5 ✉ Via dei Palchetti 6r ☎ 055 210 916 ⏰ Tue–Fri 7pm–10.30pm, Sat–Sun 12.30–2.30, 7–10.30 🚌 C1, C3

PASZKOWSKI (€€–€€€)

paszkowski.it

On the grandiose Piazza della Repubblica, this is a lovely, if expensive, old-world café and tearoom which is a great spot for people-watching. A piano bar adds a note of refinement.

➕ F5 ✉ Piazza della Repubblica 35r ⏰ Daily 7am–1am ☎ 055 210 236 🚌 C2

PERCHÉ NO! (€)

"Why not!" has to be a good name for an ice-cream place. Founded in 1939, this shop still produces plenty of new tastes to get excited about. It is renowned for its *semifreddi*, which come in creamy tastes such as hazelnut mousse and *zuppa inglese* (trifle).

➕ F6 ✉ Via dei Tavolini 19r ☎ 055 239 8969 ⏰ Wed–Mon noon–8 🚌 C2

IL PIZZAIUOLO (€)

ilpizzaiuolo.com

For great pizza, try this white-tiled restaurant where the Neapolitan-style pizzas (with puffy crusts) are baked in a wood-burning oven. The menu includes pasta dishes and delicious desserts too—try a Neapolitan rum baba.

➕ H6 ✉ Via de' Macci 113r ☎ 055 241 171 🕐 Mon–Sat 12.30–3, 5–midnight 🚊 C2, C3

PROCACCI (€–€€)

procacci1885.it

This delightful bar is something of a legend because of its *panini tartufati*, sandwiches made with a white truffle puree—just the thing to accompany a glass of prosecco.

➕ E5 ✉ Via de' Tornabuoni 64r 🕐 Mon–Sat 10–9, Sun 11–8 ☎ 055 211 656 🚊 C2

RIVOIRE (€€–€€€)

rivoire.it

This café, opened in the 1870s, is a Florentine institution. At Rivoire, you pay for the view, but it's well worth the money. Set on the Piazza della Signoria, looking out toward the Palazzo Vecchio, this is the ideal place to relax after a hectic visit to the Uffizi.

➕ F6 ✉ Piazza della Signoria 5r ☎ 055 214 412 🕐 Summer Tue–Sun 7.30am–midnight; winter Tue–Sun 7.30am–9pm 🚊 C1, C3, D

SE.STO ON ARNO (€€€)

sestoonarno.com

The glass walls on the rooftop at SE.STO give you 360-degree views over the city and beyond, making it an ideal setting for a romantic celebration dinner. Marco Lorenzini's sophisticated, French-inspired cooking lives up to the setting with creative menus featuring fish, seafood and game.

➕ D5 ✉ Piazza Ognissanti 3 ☎ 055 2715 2783 🕐 Daily 12.30–2.30, 7.30–10.30 🚊 C3

SOSTANZA (€€)

Also known as Il Troia, this ex-butcher's shop is a classic, popular with locals and tourists who all come for the famous *tortino di carciofi* (a kind of artichoke omelette) and chicken breast sautéed in butter. The *bistecca alla Fiorentina* is good too. You may have to share your table with other diners here.

➕ E5 ✉ Via del Porcellana 25r ☎ 055 212 691 🕐 Mon–Fri 12.30–2, 7.30–11 🚊 C3, 6, 11

VIVOLI (€)

vivoli.it

Vivoli is legendary; the family have been making ice cream since the 1930s. If you don't mind the wait, the rewards are delicious. There are lots of tempting choices, including an extra creamy *mousse di amaretto*, all served in *coppette* (cups)—Vivoli is strictly a no-cone zone.

➕ G6 ✉ Via Isola delle Stinche 7r ☎ 055 292 334 🕐 Apr–Oct Tue–Sat 7.30am–midnight, Sun 9am–midnight; Nov–Mar Tue–Sat 7.30am–9pm, Sun 9–9 🚊 C2

WINTER GARDEN BY CAINO (€€€)

wintergardenbycaino.com

The lavish interior of the restaurant at the grand St. Regis Florence hotel (▷ 112) is a fitting setting for Gentian Shehi's Michelin-starred food. His well-balanced menus are rooted in Tuscan culinary heritage while allowing for a flourish of creativity.

➕ D5 ✉ St. Regis Florence, Piazza Ognissanti 1 ☎ 055 2716 3770 🕐 Daily 11–11 🚊 C3

STAND OR SIT

You will almost always pay a premium to sit down and to enjoy the privilege of waiter service at coffee shops, cafés and *gelaterie* that often double up as all-round bars to be enjoyed during the day. If you stand, which is less expensive, you are generally not expected to linger too long after finishing your refreshment.

The North Centro

The area of the city fanning out northwards from the Duomo is a district abundant with fine churches, the epitome of which is the magnificent domed cathedral itself.

Via Salvestrina

Palazzo
Pandolfini

Gallo

Casino
Mediceo

VIA

CAVOUR

Via d. Dogana

Via

Via Pier Antonio

Via

Via Luigi Cherubini

Venezia

VIALE

GIACOMO

Capponi

Michell

P

MATTEOTTI

San
Marco

Gen M
Fanti

Piazza
San Marco

P

Galleria
dell'Accademia

Via

Ricasoli

Via Giorgio La Pira

Giardino
dei Semplici

Museo di Storia
Naturale-Botanica

Via Cesare Battisti

Università

Santissima
Annunziata

Piazza d. Ss
Annunziata

Ferdinando I

Via G. Fibbiai

Via Alfani

Museo
Archeologico

Orno

Giardino
della
Gherardesca

Palazzo
Capponi

Via

PINTI

Via Laura

Piazzale
Donatello

Cimitero
degli Inglesi

Museo di
Leonardo
da Vinci

Piazza
Brunelleschi

Via dei Castellacci

degli

Via della Pergola

Ospedale
d Innocenti

Via Laura

BORGO

Giuseppe

Palazzo
Panciatichi-Ximenes

P

Via V. Alfieri

Giusti

VIALE

ANTONIO

Via della Mattonaia

GRAMSCI

Ospedale
S Maria Nuova

Via Bufalini

Via dell'Oriuolo

Piazza di
Santa Maria
Nuova

P

Via del Pergola

Teatro d
Pergola

Santa Maria
Maddalena
dei Pazzi

Afrani

Colonna

PINTI

BORGO

Via Fiesolana

Crocifissione
del Perugino

Via Ge.

P

Via L. C. Farini

Piazza
Massimo
D'Azeglio

Via P. Giordani

Via dello Stecco

P

Museo Nazionale
di Antropologia
e Etnologia

Via dei Pepi

Via di

Via dei

Pilastri

Mezzo

Sinagoga

Via G. Carducci

Via G B Niccolini

Via
C Leopardi

i

Borgo degli Albizi

Piazza
G Salvemini

G

H

J

Battistero

HIGHLIGHTS

- 13th-century mosaics of the *Last Judgement*
- Ghiberti's east doors
- Pisano's south doors
- Zodiac pavement
- Romanesque marble exterior

Perhaps the best loved of all Florence's edifices is the beautiful octagonal Baptistery referred to by Dante as his "*bel* San Giovanni," and dedicated to the city's patron saint, St. John the Baptist.

Roman origins The Baptistery is one of the oldest buildings in the city. Remains of a Roman palace lie under it, and the present construction dates from somewhere between the fifth and seventh centuries AD. For many centuries it was the place where Florentines were baptized and it is clear where the font stood until its removal in 1576.

Rich ornament The entire outer surface is covered with beautiful white and green marble, added between the 11th and 13th centuries.

From left: The entire inside of the dome is covered with tiers of intricate 13th-century mosaics, depicting biblical scenes with a large Christ in the centre; the Battistero viewed from the Campanile

Inside, the ceiling is encrusted with stunning mosaics. Above the altar, designs show the Virgin and St. John the Baptist; the main design depicts the *Last Judgement*, with the sinful being devoured by diabolical creatures while the virtuous ascend to heaven. The tessellated floor is almost Islamic in its intricate geometry.

Bronze doors The Baptistery is renowned, above all, for its bronze doors: the south doors, by Pisano (1336), and Ghiberti's north and east doors (1403–24 and 1425–52). The east doors, referred to by Michelangelo as the "Gates of Paradise," are divided into 10 panels depicting Old Testament scenes. In 1990 copies of these doors replaced the originals, which are on view in the Museo dell'Opera del Duomo (▷ 62).

THE BASICS

operaduomo.firenze.it

✚ F5

✉ Piazza San Giovanni

☎ 055 230 2885

🕐 Apr–Sep Mon–Sat 8.15–10.15, 11.15–7.30, Sun 8.15–1.30; Oct–Mar Mon–Sat 11.15–7.30, Sun 11.15–1

🚇 C1, C2

♿ Good

💶 Moderate; joint ticket with Duomo and Campanile expensive

Campanile

TOP
25

The superb bell tower affords fantastic views of the city—the climb is worth the effort

THE BASICS

operaduomofirenze.it
+ F5
✉ Piazza del Duomo
☎ 055 230 2885
🕐 Daily 8.30–7.30 (last admission 40 min before closing)
🚌 C1, C2
♿ Non-existent; no elevator; 414 steps
💰 Expensive

HIGHLIGHTS

● Views from the top
● Reliefs by Pisano and della Robbia

Tall and beautifully proportioned, the bell tower of the Duomo is one of the loveliest in Italy and adds a calm and graceful note to the otherwise busy cathedral complex.

Multiple effort The Campanile, or bell tower, of the Duomo rises to 85m (279ft). It was begun in 1334 and finished in 1359. Giotto was involved in its design, but by the time of his death in 1337 only the base was in place. Andrea Pisano completed the second floor and the tower was finished by Francesco Talenti.

Relief sculpture The outside is decorated in the same polychrome marble as the Duomo: white marble from Carrara, green marble from Prato and pink marble from the Maremma. Around the bottom are two sets of relief sculptures: the lower tier is in hexagonal panels, the upper tier in diamonds. What you see are in fact copies; the originals have been moved to the Museo dell'Opera del Duomo (▷ 62) to protect them. The reliefs in the hexagonal panels, which were executed by Pisano (although some are believed to have been designed by Giotto), show the Creation of Man, the Arts and the Industries. On the north face are the five Liberal Arts (grammar, philosophy, music, arithmetic and astrology), executed by Luca della Robbia. The upper tier of reliefs, also by Pisano, illustrates the Seven Planets, the Seven Virtues and the Liberal Arts; the Seven Sacraments are attributed to Alberto Arnoldi.

Madonna and Child
*by Michelangelo (left);
Cappella dei Principi
(right)*

Cappelle Medicee

The monumental tomb complex of the Medici perfectly illustrates the family's power and wealth, while Michelangelo's sublime sculpture is among the most important artistic legacies in the city.

Burial places The mausoleum of the Medici family is in three distinct parts of the church of San Lorenzo (▷ 64): the crypt, the Cappella dei Principi and the Sagrestia Nuova. The crypt was where the bodies of minor members of the dynasty were unceremoniously dumped. Tidied up in the 19th century, it now houses tomb slabs. The Cappella dei Principi has a huge dome by Bernado Buontalenti, begun in 1604 and not completed until the 20th century. The inner surface is decorated in a heavy, grandiose way with the Medici coat of arms everywhere. The tombs of six Medici Grand Dukes are in the chapel beneath the dome.

New Sacristy Right of the altar, the Sagrestia Nuova, built by Michelangelo between 1520 and 1534, is a reminder that the Medici were enlightened patrons. Michelangelo sculpted figures representing *Night and Day*, and *Dawn and Dusk* to adorn the tombs of Lorenzo, Duke of Urbino (1492–1519), and Giuliano, Duke of Nemours (1479–1516). The figure of *Night*, with moon, owl and mask, is one of his finest works. The *Madonna and Child* (1521) is by Michelangelo as well. In a room left of the altar are some superb charcoal drawings found in 1975 and attributed to Michelangelo.

THE BASICS

bargellomusei.beniculturali.it
🔢 F5
✉ Piazza Madonna degli Aldobrandini 6
🕐 Daily 8.15–1.50 (last admission 30 min before closing); closed 1st, 3rd, 5th Mon and 2nd, 4th Sun of month
🚆 C1, C2
♿ Poor; ask for assistance
💶 Moderate
❓ English audio guides (moderate)

HIGHLIGHTS

● Michelangelo's *Night*
● The figure of Lorenzo, Duke of Urbino
● Michelangelo's *Madonna and Child*
● Sketches attributed to Michelangelo
● Charcoal drawings by Michelangelo

Duomo

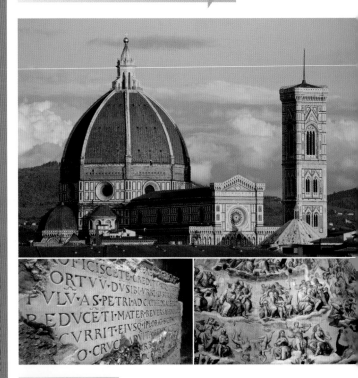

HIGHLIGHTS

● Brunelleschi's dome
● Santa Reparata remains
● Uccello's mural to a
14th-century Captain-
General

TIPS

● You will not be allowed
into the Duomo wearing
a sleeveless top or
skimpy shorts.
● The only way up the
Dome is to climb 463 steep,
narrow steps—this is not
for the claustrophobic.

The huge bulk of the Duomo, surmounted by its iconic dome, dominates the city skyline. The ornate polychrome marble of the exterior contrasts superbly with the simple lines of the cupola, with its white ribs and terracotta tiles.

Long-term build The cathedral of Santa Maria del Fiori, the Florence Duomo, is a vast Gothic structure built on the site of the seventh-century church of Santa Reparata, whose remains lie in the crypt. It was built at the end of the 13th century, although the colossal dome was not added until the 15th century, and the facade was not finished until the 19th century. The exterior is a decorative riot of pink, white and green marble; by contrast the interior is stark and plain. The clock above the entrance on the

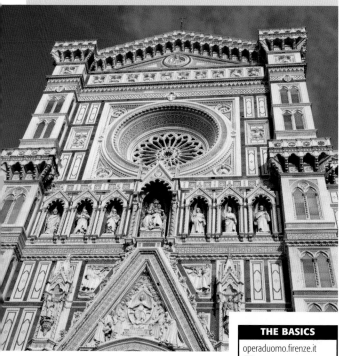

Clockwise from left: The Duomo with its Renaissance tiled dome and adjacent bell tower; the highly decorated neo-Gothic facade was completed in 1887; Vasari's frescoes of the *Last Judgement*; the crypt has remains from Roman times and the early Christian church of Santa Reparata

west wall inside was designed by Paolo Uccello in 1443, in line with the *ora italica*, according to which the 24th hour of the day ends at sunset.

Roman influences Built by Brunelleschi, who won the competition for its commission in 1418, the dome was made without scaffolding. The best way to see the dome is to climb up it. The route takes you through the interior, where you can see Vasari's much-reviled frescoes of the *Last Judgement* (1572–79), and toward the lantern, from where the views are fantastic.

Explosion At Easter the *Scoppio del Carro*, a traditional costume parade followed by Mass in the Duomo, culminates with a mechanical dove being launched from the high altar along a wire through the entrance, igniting a cart of fireworks.

THE BASICS

operaduomo.firenze.it

🚻 F5

✉ Piazza del Duomo

☎ 055 230 2885

🕐 Cathedral Mon–Wed, Fri 10–5, Thu 10–4 (till 5 Jul–Sep, till 4.30 Nov–Apr), Sat 10–4.45, Sun 1.30–4.45. Dome (access from Porta della Mandoria) Mon–Fri 8.30–7, Sat 8.30–5.40 (last admission 40 min before closing)

🚌 C1, C2

♿ Good (access via Porta di Canonica, south side), except for Dome

✋ Free; dome expensive; crypt moderate

Galleria dell'Accademia

- Michelangelo's *David*
- Michelangelo's *Prisoners*
- Giambologna's *Rape of the Sabine Women*
- Buonaguida's *Tree of Life*

TIP

- If you want to view *David*, arrive when the museum first opens, or late in the day, to avoid the long queues.

Michelangelo's *David*, exhibited in the Accademia, has a powerful impact: the intensity of his gaze, that assured posture, those huge hands, the anatomical precision of the veins and the muscles.

Art school The Accademia was founded in 1784 to teach techniques of painting, drawing and sculpture. Since 1873 it has housed the world's single most important collection of sculptures by Michelangelo. There are also sculptures by other artists, as well as many paintings, mostly from the Renaissance period.

Masterpiece The main attraction is *David* by Michelangelo, sculpted in 1504 and exhibited outside the Palazzo Vecchio until 1873, when it was transferred to the Accademia to protect it

From left: Gothic alterpieces from late 14th-century Florence in the upstairs hall; the most famous and most visited of all statues in Florence, Michelangelo's magnificent sculpture of David

from environmental damage. It captures the moment at which the young David contemplates defying the giant Goliath.

Freedom from stone The *Prisoners* (1505) was made for the tomb of Pope Julius II. The title refers to Michelangelo's belief that when he sculpted a statue, he was freeing the figure from the marble, and the style, particularly preferred by Michelangelo, was called the *non finito* (unfinished). After his death, the *Prisoners* was moved to the Grotta Grande in the Boboli Gardens (▷ 82), where the originals were replaced with casts in 1908. Also seek out the original plaster model for *The Rape of the Sabine Women* (1583), Giambologna's last work; the marble version is in the Loggia dei Lanzi in Piazza della Signoria (▷ 32).

THE BASICS

galleriaaccademiafirenze.
beniculturali.it

➕ G4

✉ Via Ricasoli 58–60

☎ 055 098 7100.
Firenzecard holders should
call 055 294 883 to book.
Advance booking is
mandatory

🕐 Tue–Sun 8.15–6.50;
Apr–Sep Tue and Thu till
10pm; closed 1 May

🚌 C1, C2

♿ Good

💶 Expensive

Museo dell'Opera del Duomo

TOP 25

Detail of a dancing choir by Lucca della Robbia (left); a fresco in the museum (right)

THE BASICS

operaduomo.firenze.it

✚ G5

✉ Piazza del Duomo 9

☎ 055 230 2885

🕐 Daily 9–7.30 (Sun till 1.45); closed first Tue of month

🚌 C1, C2

♿ Good

💰 Expensive

HIGHLIGHTS

● Singing galleries
● Original panels from the Campanile
● Michelangelo's *Pietà*
● Original panels from the "Gates of Paradise"
● Donatello's *Maddalena*

Founded, and still functioning as, the workshop for cathedral repairs, the Museo dell'Opera is also home today to superb artistic treasures from the buildings that comprise the cathedral complex.

Refuge from pollution This workshop and museum was founded when the Duomo was built, to maintain the art of the cathedral. Its location was chosen in the 15th century, and it was in its courtyard that Michelangelo sculpted his *David*. Since 1891 it has housed works from the cathedral complex, leaving the Duomo rather empty of art.

Michelangelo's *Pietà* On the first level you can see eight of the original 10 bronze panels from the east door of the Baptistery by Lorenzo Ghiberti. On the main landing is the *Pietà* (begun c.1550) by Michelangelo. It is said he intended it for his own tomb; the hooded figure of Nicodemus is often interpreted as a self-portrait. The damage to Christ's left leg and arm is believed to have been inflicted by Michelangelo in frustration at his failing skills.

Artists compared The main room on the first floor contains two *cantorie* (singing galleries) that once stood in the Duomo: one by Luca della Robbia (1431–38), the other by Donatello (1433–39). In the room on the left are panels by Pisano from the Campanile (▷ 56); next door are construction materials and instruments used for Brunelleschi's dome.

The Hall of Mirrors has a frescoed ceiling by Luca Giordano (left); the garden (right)

Palazzo Medici-Riccardi

The Medici family ruled Florence with a combination of tyranny and humanity, and this is reflected in the imposing facade of their huge headquarters, with its fearsome lattice of window bars.

Medici origins The Palazzo Medici-Riccardi, now mostly government offices, was the seat of the Medici family from its completion in 1444 until 1540, when Cosimo I moved the Medici residence to the Palazzo Vecchio and this palace was bought by the Riccardi family.

Setting a trend The palace design, by Michelozzo, was widely imitated in Florence, for example in the Palazzo Strozzi and the Palazzo Pitti (▷ 84–85). It is characterized by huge slabs of stone with a rough-hewn, rustic appearance. The courtyard is in a lighter style, with a graceful colonnade and black and white *sgraffito* decoration of medallions, based on Roman intaglios collected by the Medici and displayed in the Museo degli Argenti (▷ 85).

A regal scene Steps right of the entrance lead to the Cappella dei Magi. This tiny chapel has the dazzling fresco cycle depicting the *Journey of the Magi* (1459–63) that Piero de' Medici commissioned from Gozzoli in memory of the Compagnia dei Magi, a religious organization to which the Medici belonged. Portraits of the Medici are believed to have been incorporated into the characters, while the procession recalls the pageantry of the Compagnia dei Magi.

THE BASICS

palazzo-medici.it

➕ F5

✉ Via Cavour 3

☎ 055 276 8224

🕐 Thu–Tue 8.30–7 (last admission 6.30)

🚌 C1, C2

♿ Entrance on Via Cavour; Cappella poor

💶 Moderate

❓ Entrance to chapel limited to 15 people at a time every 15 min

HIGHLIGHTS

● Gozzoli's fresco cycle of the *Journey of the Magi* (1459–63)
● Courtyard

San Lorenzo

TOP 25

The facade of Basilica di San Lorenzo (left); the cloisters (right)

THE BASICS

✚ F5

✉ Piazza San Lorenzo

☎ 055 216 634.
Biblioteca Laurenziana 055 293 7911; bml.firenze.sbn.it

🕐 Mon–Sat 10–5.
Biblioteca Mon, Wed, Fri 8–2, Tue, Thu 8–5.30

🚌 C1, C2

♿ Poor

💶 Moderate

HIGHLIGHTS

● Biblioteca Laurenziana (begun 1524)
● Staircase by Michelangelo
● Bronzino's *Martyrdom of St. Lawrence*
● Pulpits by Donatello
● Brunelleschi's Sagrestia Vecchia

San Lorenzo is the parish church and burial place of the Medici and is filled with art commissioned by them. As with the Cappelle Medicee, it is a monument to the family's artistic patronage.

A sacred site San Lorenzo was rebuilt by Filippo Brunelleschi between 1425 and 1446, on the site of one of the city's oldest churches (consecrated in AD393). Its rough-hewn ochre exterior was to have been covered with a facade by Michelangelo. This was never added, but a model is in Casa Buonarroti (▷ 37). A modern statue of Anna Maria Luisa (*d.*1743), the last of the Medici dynasty, stands rather incongruously at the base of the campanile. The church, with its *pietra serena* (grey sandstone) columns, is cool and airy, with bronze pulpits (*c.*1460) depicting the Resurrection and scenes from the life of Christ, Donatello's last work. Bronzino's fresco (facing the altar, left), the *Martyrdom of St. Lawrence* (1569), is an absorbing Mannerist study of the human body in various contortions. Inside the Sagrestia Vecchia (Old Sacristy, 1421) are eight *tondi* (circular reliefs) by Donatello depicting the evangelists and scenes from the life of St. John.

Biblioteca Laurenziana The Laurentian Library houses the Medici's collection of manuscripts (not on display). This extraordinary example of Mannerist architecture by Michelangelo is left of the church, up a curvaceous *pietra serena* staircase via the cloisters.

The Annuncication
*by Fra Angelico (left);
the ornate exterior
of San Marco (right)*

TOP
25

San Marco

Dominated by the lovely paintings of Fra Angelico, the soothing convent of San Marco has an aura of monastic calm that is conducive to appreciating the religious themes depicted.

Medici motives San Marco was founded in the 13th century by Silvestrine monks. In 1437 Cosimo il Vecchio invited the Dominican monks of Fiesole to move into the convent and had it rebuilt by Michelozzo, a gesture motivated by his guilt for his wealth from banking and by the fact that the Dominicans were useful allies. Ironically, Savonarola, who denounced the decadence of the Medici at the end of the 15th century, came to prominence as the Dominican prior of San Marco.

A feast for the eyes The Chiostro di Sant' Antonino, the cloister through which you enter, is decorated with faded frescoes by Fra Angelico and other Florentine artists. In the Ospizio dei Pellegrini, where pilgrims were cared for, there is a superb collection of paintings by Fra Angelico and his followers. At the top of the staircase on the way to the dormitory is Fra Angelico's *Annunciation* (1440), an image of great tenderness and grace. Each of the 44 monks' cells is adorned with a small fresco by Fra Angelico or one of his assistants. The themes include the *Entombment* (cell 2) and the *Mocking of Christ* (cell 7). Cells 38 and 39 were reserved for Cosimo il Vecchio, who periodically spent time in the monastery.

THE BASICS

polomusealetoscana.
beniculturali.it

⊞ G4

✉ Piazza San Marco 3

☎ 055 088 2000

🕐 Church daily 7–12, 4–8. Museum Mon–Fri 8.30–1.50, Sat–Sun 8.15–4.50; closed 1st, 3rd, 5th Sun, 2nd and 4th Mon of month

🚌 C1

♿ Acceptable

✋ Moderate

HIGHLIGHTS

● Fra Angelico's cell paintings
● Fra Angelico's *Annunciation*
● Savonarola's cells
● Cosimo il Vecchio's cells

Santa Maria Novella

S-curved volute (left) on the upper part of the facade of Santa Maria Novella (right)

THE BASICS

smn.it

🔢 E5

✉ Piazza di Santa Maria Novella

☎ 055 219 257

🕐 Apr–Sep Sat–Thu 9–7, Fri 11–7; Oct–Mar Sat–Thu 9–5.30, Fri 11–5.30 (last admission 45 min before closing)

🚶 5-min walk from the railway station

🚌 All buses to train station

♿ Good

💶 Church inexpensive; museum inexpensive

HIGHLIGHTS

● Marble facade
● Masaccio's *Trinita*
● Cappellone degli Spagnoli
● Tornabuoni Chapel
● Brunelleschi's wooden crucifix (1420) in Cappella Gondi

This Gothic church, with its wonderful black and white facade, is packed with artistic treasures and lovely stained glass, while its beautiful cloisters are decorated with frescoes by Paolo Uccello.

Dominican origins Santa Maria Novella was built between 1279 and 1357 by Dominican monks. The lower part of the marble facade, Romanesque in style, is believed to be by Fra Jacopo Talenti; the upper part was completed in the 15th century by Leon Battista Alberti.

Deceptive interior Inside, the vast church looks even longer than it is, thanks to the clever spacing of the columns. As you face the altar, on the left-hand side is Masaccio's fresco of the *Trinita* (c.1428), one of the earliest paintings to demonstrate mastery of perspective. Many of the chapels are named after the church's wealthy patrons. The Strozzi Chapel (left transept) is dedicated to St. Thomas Aquinas and decorated with frescoes (1351–57) depicting *Heaven and Hell*: Dante himself is represented in the *Last Judgement* just behind the altar. The Tornabuoni Chapel contains Ghirlandaio's fresco cycle of the life of St. John the Baptist (1485) in contemporary costume. The Cappellone degli Spagnoli was used by the courtiers of Eleanor of Toledo, wife of Cosimo I. In the frescoes *Triumph of the Doctrine* (c.1365) by Andrea da Firenze, the dogs of God (a pun on Dominican—*domini canes*) are sent to round up lost sheep into the fold of the church.

Detail of Pietro Tacca's fountain (left) in Piazza Santissima Annunziata (right)

Santissima Annunziata

The lovely piazza of SS Annunziata offers superb architecture on an intimate scale, the 15th-century church perfectly balanced by the arcades of the Ospedale degli Innocenti and the building opposite.

Old New Year The Feast of the Annunciation on 25 March used to be New Year in the old Florentine calendar, and the church and the square have always played a special role in the life of the city. Every year a fair is still held in the square on that date.

Wedding flowers The church of Santissima Annunziata was built by Michelozzo between 1444 and 1481 on the site of a Servite oratory. A portico leads to the Chiostrino dei Voti, superbly frescoed by Andrea del Sarto, while the interior contains fine Mannerist works. The church is dedicated to the Virgin Mary, due to the legend that a painting of the Virgin was started by a monk in 1252 and finished by an angel. Newlyweds have traditionally brought their wedding bouquet to the church to ensure a happy marriage.

Early orphanage The Ospedale degli Innocenti, on the east side of the piazza, was the first orphanage in Europe. A small museum, completely overhauled in 2016, includes works by major artists from the 14th to the 18th centuries. Designed by Brunelleschi in 1419, its graceful portico is decorated with enamel terracotta roundels by della Robbia (1498).

THE BASICS

➕ G4
✉ Piazza della SS. Annunziata
☎ 055 266 181; Ospedale 055 203 7308; museodeglinnocenti.it
🕐 Daily 7.30–12.30, 4–6.30; closed during services. Ospedale daily 10–7
🚌 C1
♿ Good
💶 Church free; Ospedale moderate

HIGHLIGHTS

● Andrea della Robbia's roundels
● Facade of the Ospedale degli Innocenti
● Rosso Fiorentino's *Assumption*
● Pontormo's *Visitation*
● Andrea del Sarto's *Birth of the Virgin*

More to See

GIARDINO DEI SEMPLICI

This oasis of neat greenery, the botanical garden of Florence University, is on the site of a garden laid out in 1545–46 for Cosimo I and is named after the medicinal plants (*semplici*) grown here. Today it holds around 6,000 plants and has greenhouses with tropical palms, orchids and citrus fruits.
� G4 ✉ Via Micheli 3 ☎ 055 275 6794 🕐 Apr–Sep Tue–Fri 10–7; Oct–Mar Sat–Sun 10–4 🚍 C1 ♿ Good 💶 Inexpensive

MERCATO CENTRALE

mercatocentrale.it
The largest of Florence's produce markets is held here in Giuseppe Mengoni's magnificent cast-iron structure, which was built in 1874, with an extra floor added in 1980. The upper floor is a vibrant food hall showcasing the very best of Italian produce.
🟝 F4 ✉ Via dell'Ariento 🕐 Ground floor Jul–Aug Mon–Sat 7–2; Sep–Jun Mon–Fri 7–2, Sat 7–5. Top floor daily 10am–midnight 🚍 C1, C2, C4 ♿ Good (but crowded)

MERCATO SAN LORENZO

Fun, touristy and centrally located behind the Mercato Centrale, this market is known for its bargain leather goods. Much of what you will find is genuinely good value, but there are also cheap rip-offs.
🟝 F5 ✉ Piazza del Mercato Centrale, Via dell'Ariento 🕐 Daily 9–7.30 🚍 C1, C2 ♿ Good

MUSEO ARCHEOLOGICO

polomusealetoscana.beniculturali.it
This is one of the best places to see Etruscan art. There are also Roman, Greek and Egyptian exhibits, as well as a rare collection from Kafiri, north Pakistan.
🟝 G4 ✉ Palazzo della Crocetta, Via della Colonna 36 ☎ 055 235 75 🕐 Tue–Fri 8.30–7, Sat–Mon 8.30–2 🚍 C1 ♿ Good 💶 Moderate

MUSEO DI LEONARDO DA VINCI

mostredileonardo.com
This exhibition complex displays some 40 models of Leonardo's inventions. Categories cover

Mercato Centrale

machines connected to earth, fire, water and air, with a fifth section on mechanical devices. Visitors can try out the reconstructed machines.

➕ G5 ✉ Via dei Servi 66–68 ☎ 055 282 966 🕐 Apr–Oct daily 10–7; Nov–Mar daily 10–6 🚇 C1 ♿ Good 💶 Expensive

MUSEO NAZIONALE DI ANTROPOLOGIA E ETNOLOGIA

msn.unifi.it

Part of Florence University, this museum focuses on objects used by peoples from all over the world, ranging from a fabulous ibis feather cloak from South America to rare kimonos from Japan and trophy skulls from New Guinea.

➕ G5 ✉ Palazzo Nonfinito, Via del Proconsolo 12 ☎ 055 275 6444 🕐 Jul–Aug Tue–Thu 9–7, Fri–Sun 9–1; Sep–Jun Tue–Sun 9–5 🚇 C1, C2 ♿ Good 💶 Moderate

MUSEO DI STORIA NATURALE—BOTANICA

msn.unifi.it

The botanical collection of the Museum of Natural History (part of Florence University) houses 4 million specimens—the largest collection of its kind in Italy. Don't miss the Andrea Cesalpino Herbarium, Bartolomeo Bimbi's 17th-century still-life paintings and the superb wax models of plants.

➕ G4 ✉ Via La Pira 4 ☎ 055 275 7462 🕐 By appointment only; call first 🚇 C2 ♿ Good 💶 Free

SANTA MARIA MADDALENA DEI PAZZI

Although the original church dates from the 13th century, most of the present building was rebuilt at the end of the 15th century, designed by Giuliano da Sangallo. The spectacular interior decoration, with its marble and *trompe l'oeil*, dates from the baroque period. The highlight here is in the fresco of the 1490s by Perugino in the chapter house (reached via the crypt).

➕ H5 ✉ Borgo Pinti 58 ☎ 055 247 8420 🕐 Daily 9–12, 4.30–6.30; chapter house Tue, Thu 2.30–5.30 🚇 C2, C3 ♿ Poor 💶 Inexpensive

Trompe l'oeil *in Santa Maria Maddalena dei Pazzi*

A large painted mummy case in the Museo Archeologico

North of the City

Take in Florence's main market area and the most important churches and galleries in the northern part of the city.

DISTANCE: 3km (2 miles) **ALLOW:** Full morning

THE NORTH CENTRO WALK

START

CAPPELLE MEDICEE (▷ 57)
F5 C1, C2

END

SANTISSIMA ANNUNZIATA (▷ 67)
G4 C1

1 Start at the Cappelle Medicee (▷ 57), in Piazza Madonna degli Aldobrandini, the last resting place of many of the Medici family.

2 The church of San Lorenzo (▷ 64) itself (entered from Piazza San Lorenzo) is a masterpiece of Renaissance church design. Inside are works by Donatello.

3 Explore the market north of San Lorenzo; cut through the Mercato Centrale (▷ 68) and return to Piazza San Lorenzo. The Palazzo Medici-Riccardi (▷ 63) is on the north side.

4 Follow Via Cavour and take the second left into Via degli Arazzieri; follow into Via XXVII Aprile to reach the former convent of Sant' Apollonia, with a fresco of the Last Supper by Andrea del Castagno.

8 Across the square is the Ospedale degli Innocenti (▷ 67). If time permits, go inside to see the modest museum and the two Brunelleschi cloisters.

7 This is one of the city's most distinctive squares. The square's church, Santissima Annunziata (▷ 67), is known for its frescoes by Andrea del Sarto and others.

6 On the north side of the square, the convent of San Marco (▷ 65) is devoted to the works of Fra Angelico. Continue eastward along Via Cesare Battisti to Piazza della Santissima Annunziata.

5 Walk east to Piazza San Marco, viewing Michelangelo's *David* in the Galleria dell'Accademia (▷ 60–61).

Shopping

ALESSI

enotecaalessi.it

With some 2,500 labels to choose from, the Alessi family's shop is an excellent place to stock up on wines from Tuscany and beyond, plus teas and coffees, confectionary, jams and other goodies.
➕ F5 ✉ Via delle Oche 27r ☎ 055 214 966 🚋 C1, C2

ALICE'S MASKS ART STUDIO

alicemasks.com

Papier-mâché in all shapes and sizes is here: animals—mythical and real—as well as more theatrical and surreal characters. They are all hand painted and finished.
➕ E4 ✉ Via Faenza 72r 🚋 C2

BARTOLINI

dinobartolini.it

This Florentine institution sells just about every item of kitchenware you could wish for, as well as fine china and porcelain. All the international names are here but look out for the Italian ceramics such as Solimene-Vietri ware.
➕ G5 ✉ Via dei Servi 72r ☎ 055 291 497 🚋 C1

LA BOTTEGHINA DEL CERAMISTA

labotteghinadelceramista.it

The vivid patterns that are hand painted on the jugs, bowls and dishes at this shop will brighten any table.
➕ F4 ✉ Via Guelfa 5r ☎ 055 287 367 🚋 C2, D

CASA DEL VINO

casadelvino.it

This wine shop has occupied the same premises since it first opened in the second half of the 19th century. Today it has a very well-stocked cellar with nearly 1,000 wines from around the world. You are invited to sample wine by the glass and have a snack while deciding which bottle to buy.
➕ F4 ✉ Via dell'Ariento 16r ☎ 055 215 609 🚋 C2, D

CORNICI CAMPANI

This artisan shop has been dedicated to handcrafting picture frames since 1889. The founder, Gino Campani, was a well-known collector and celebrated frame maker. Custom-made frames take approximately one week to complete.
➕ G5 ✉ Via dei Servi 22r ☎ 055 216 984 🚋 C1

DR VRANJES

drvranjes.it

Best known for his room scents, which are presented in beautiful glass bottles with names such as "Boboli Gardens," Paolo Vranjes has several shops in Florence. His candles, body lotions and bath oils are delicious too.
➕ G3 ✉ Via San Gallo 63 ☎ 055 494 537 🚋 C1, 1, 11

EATALY

eataly.net

The Florence branch of Eataly, the food emporium that showcases the very best of Italian produce, offers an incredible assortment of food and drink, from pasta and olive oils to sweets and wine. It's open daily until 10.30.
➕ F5 ✉ Via Martelli 22r ☎ 055 015 360 🚋 C1

MARBLED PAPER

The skill of marbling paper was brought to Florence from Venice, where it had been learned from the East in the 12th century. Today's Florentine paper goods range greatly in price and quality, but even the inexpensive goods are attractive.

FRETTE

frette.com

This world-famous Italian company produces refined fabrics for the home, always at the cutting edge of fashion—bedding, tableware and lots more.

✚ G4 ✉ Via Cavour 2r ☎ 055 211 369 🚌 C1

INTIMISSIMI

The simple cotton and silk lingerie and sleepwear is hard to beat in terms of quality and price. There are four stores in central Florence

✚ E5 ✉ Via de Cerretani 15r ☎ 055 239 9132 🚌 C2

LIBRERIA ANTIQUARIA GONNELLI

gonnelli.it

For more than a century collectors have been coming to this historic bookshop to discover old and rare books, stamps and manuscripts.

✚ H4 ✉ Piazza Massimo d'Azeglio ☎ 055 216 835 🚌 C1, C2

LORETTA CAPONI

lorettacaponi.com

Loretta Caponi's store is filled with hand-embroidered table linens, nightclothes and lingerie for mother and daughter, and silk pyjamas for men. It's a good source of wedding presents.

✚ E5 ✉ Piazza Antinori 4r ☎ 055 213 668 🚌 C2

MANDRAGORA ARTSTORE

mandragora.it

Mandragora stocks an excellent range of arty books, postcards and prints, as well as an above-average selection of gift items such as T-shirts, mugs and calendars. There's a choice for kids, too.

✚ F5 ✉ Piazza del Duomo 50r ☎ 055 292 559 🚌 C1, C2

SHOE CITY

The Florentines are famed for making superb shoes. As a testament to the historical importance of the industry in the city's economy, one of the main streets is named after the shoemakers (Calzaiuoli). The range of shoes available is vast, from the pinnacle of international chic to the value-for-money styles in San Lorenzo market. Showrooms at the leather "factories" in the Santa Croce area are worth a visit.

OSTERIA DE L'ORTOLANO

osteriafirenze.com

A must for fans of Italian food, this excellent delicatessen and catering company has been in business since 1962. Pick up a complete meal to take out or choose from the biscuits, jams and sauces for a delicious souvenir to bring home.

✚ G5 ✉ Via degli Alfani 91r ☎ 055 239 6466 🚌 C2

IL PAPIRO

ilpapirofirenze.eu

These shops (there are several branches) in central Florence sell excellent marbled paper goods in particularly pretty shades. These include little chests of drawers and tiny jewellery boxes.

✚ G4 ✉ Via Cavour 49r ☎ 055 215 262 🚌 C1

PENKO BOTTEGA ORAFA

paolopenko.com

Master goldsmith Paolo Penko makes beautiful jewellery to order using techniques and intricate designs that originate from the Renaissance period. His previous clients range from the Pope to Paris Hilton.

✚ F5 ✉ Via Ferdinando Zannetti 14–16r ☎ 055 211 661 🚌 C1

LE PIETRE NELL'ARTE

scarpellimosaici.it

From this classy shop the Scarpelli family sell beautiful hard and semiprecious stone inlays, interior decorations and artistic objects including sculptures, tables, pictures, brooches and much more. The stones used include onyx, chalcedony, malachite and jasper.

🔹 F5 ✉ Via Ricasoli 59r ☎ 055 212 587
🚍 C1, C2

RICHARD GINORI

richardginori1735.com

Florence's own porcelain designer will also make dinner services to order with your family crest, a picture of your home or whatever else you want.

🔹 E5 ✉ Via Rondinelli 17r ☎ 055 210 041 🚍 C2

SBIGOLI TERRECOTTE

sbigoliterrecotte.it

Pots here are designed, painted and fired in Florence by the family owners, whose workshop is behind the shop and can be visited. The designs, based mainly on familiar Tuscan themes such as olives or the geometric plants popular in the Renaissance, come in majolica and tactile unglazed terracotta, and at good prices.

🔹 G5 ✉ Via Sant'Egidio 4r ☎ 055 247 9713 🚍 C1

SCRIPTORIUM

atelierscriptorium.it

This shop draws on two great Florentine crafts—leather working and paper making—to create objects of beauty and refined taste. The plain paper books are notable, bound with soft leather in subdued natural shades.

🔹 G5 ✉ Via dei Pucci 4 ☎ 055 238 2620
🚍 C1

SOCIÉTÉ ANONYME

For a different fashion experience, head over to Massimiliano Gianelli's eclectic, minimalist store to hunt through international labels such as Helmut Lang and Comme des Garçons for easy-to-wear pieces with a contemporary feel.

🔹 H5 ✉ Via Giovan Battista Niccolini 3F
☎ 055 386 084 🚍 C2, C3

VESTRI

vestri.it

Vestri's handmade chocolates come flavoured with chilli, cointreau, green tea, extra virgin olive oil and much more. In winter you can indulge in sinful hot chocolate, in summer chocolate ice cream, maybe with wild strawberries.

🔹 G6 ✉ Borgo degli Albizi 11r ☎ 055 234 0374 🚍 C1, C2

ZANOBINI

lelame.com

Part traditional bar, part wine shop, Zanobini's is patronized by locals. Enjoy a snack and a chat with the friendly owners while you buy your wine.

🔹 F4 ✉ Via Sant'Antonino 47r ☎ 055 239 6850 🚍 C1

CHIANTI

Chianti gets its name from the region in which it is made. Sangiovese grapes are harvested in October, pressed and then the juice and skins of the grapes are fermented for about 15 days, after which the juice alone is given a second fermentation. In spring the wine is matured in wooden casks. Chianti Classico is usually regarded as the best of the seven types of Chianti. This is produced in the eponymous region (▷ 99) north of Siena. Wines of the Chianti Classico Consortium bear the symbol of the Gallo Nero (black cockerel).

Entertainment and Nightlife

JAZZ CLUB

Jazz aficionados flock to this popular venue for its programme of live jazz and relaxed atmosphere. Although technically a private club, it is very easy to become a member (▷ panel).

✚ H5 ✉ Via Nuova dei Caccini 3 🕔 Closed Mon, Sun and Jun–Sep 🚌 C1

THE MEDICI DYNASTY SHOW

medicidynasty.com

This multimedia show tells (in English) the 300-year story of the Medici, Florence's ruling family, through the eyes of the last family members, who left their art collections to the city.

✚ E4 ✉ Via Faenza 48 ☎ Box office 349 131 0441 🚌 All buses to station

OPERA DI FIRENZE

maggiofiorentino.com

Florence's spectacular modern opera house, with its 2,000-seater auditorium, is the main venue of the Maggio Musicale music festival in May and June, but has a full programme of opera, concerts and dance throughout the year.

✚ C5 ✉ Piazza Vittorio Gui 1 ☎ Box office 055 200 1278 🚌 C1, C2, D

CLUBS ITALIAN STYLE

Many clubs and music venues are private clubs or *associazione culturale*. This doesn't mean that visitors are unwelcome but that it's easier for them to get a licence as a club than as a public *locale*. It's very easy to become a member; you may be charged a euro or so above the official entry price, but it's still worth doing even if you're only going to use your membership once. All you need to do is fill in your name, address, date of birth and sometimes occupation on a form and you'll be presented with a membership card.

OPERA ET GUSTO

Spend an evening combining a superb meal with music, dance and theatre. The tables are arranged at the foot of the stage and red velvet curtains encircle the room, creating an intimate feel. After the performance the venue transforms into a bar with live music.

✚ E5 ✉ Via della Scala 17r ☎ 055 288 190 🕔 Show 8pm–10.45pm. Bar until 2am 🚌 C2

REX CAFÈ

rexfirenze.com

The stunning interior boasts artistic lighting, a colourful mosaic behind the bar and a life-sized marlin suspended from the ceiling. Great cocktails and good music, both DJ sessions and live, make this place ever-popular, and it stays open until 2.30am.

✚ H5 ✉ Via Fiesolana 23r ☎ 055 248 0331 🚌 C1, C2

SPACE ELECTRONIC

spaceclubfirenze.it

Upstairs you'll find a vast dance floor, where an eclectic selection of music is played, ranging from up-to-the-minute hits to 1950s and 1960s classics. It's noisy and very popular with tourists.

✚ D5 ✉ Via Palazzuolo 37 ☎ 055 293 082 🚌 D

TEATRO DELLA PERGOLA

teatrodellapergola.com

Internationally renowned musicians are regularly featured on the concert series organized by the Amici della Musica (amicidellamusica.it). Concerts are held in the glorious red and gold theatre or in the more intimate *saloncino*. This is one of the most important venues for classical music in the city.

✚ G5 ✉ Via della Pergola 12–32 ☎ 055 22641 🚌 C1, C2

Where to Eat

PRICES

Prices are approximate, based on a 3-course meal for one person.

€€€ over €60
€€ €40–€60
€ under €40

ANTELLESI (€€)

trattoriaantellesi.blogspot.com

Antellesi is a great place for a vegetarian to join a meat-eating friend. There's a good range of inventive starters and delicious main courses—the *peposo alla fiorentina* (a peppery beef stew in red wine) is very tasty. There is a decent wine list and a traditional Florentine dessert made with chestnuts.

🔳 E4 ✉ Via Faenza 9r ☎ 055 265 4616 🕐 Daily noon–midnight 🚌 C2

L'ANTICA PIZZERIA DA MICHELE (€)

pizzeriadamichelefirenze.it

Michele's pizzeria started in Naples in 1870, so the Florentine branch will give you a taste of the real thing (one of the few foods to be recognized by UNESCO as world heritage). They serve six great classics only. Try the Neapolitana—topped with tomato, mozzarella, anchovies and capers.

🔳 F4 ✉ Piazza del Mercato Centrale 22r ☎ 055 269 6173 🕐 Daily noon–11 🚌 C1

BELCORE (€€)

ristorantebelcore.it

Here you can enjoy refined modern Italian cooking in tranquil, elegant surroundings. The plain cream walls provide a stage for the work of up-and-coming artists. The impressive wine list has more than 300 wines to choose from.

🔳 D5 ✉ Via dell'Albero 30 ☎ 055 211 198 🕐 Daily 7–11.30pm 🚌 C2, D

CANTINETTA ANTINORI (€€€)

cantinetta-antinori.com

Well-heeled tourists and chic Florentines are among the regulars at this elegant restaurant, where the menus are based on classic Florentine and Tuscan dishes such as *pappa al pomodoro*, a typical bread-based tomato soup. Wines are from the renowned Antinori estates.

🔳 E5 ✉ Piazza Antinori 3 ☎ 055 292 234 🕐 Mon–Sat noon–2.30, 7–10.30. Closed Aug 🚌 C2

COQUINARIUS (€€)

coquinarius.com

This restaurant-cum-wine bar full of dark wood and stylish posters is a great place to sample different cheeses, cold cuts, smoked fish, *stuzzichini* (Italian bar snacks) and exceptionally good cakes.

🔳 F5 ✉ Via delle Oche 11r ☎ 055 230 2153 🕐 Mon–Fri 6–11pm, Sat–Sun noon–11 🚌 C1

GELATERIA CARABÉ (€)

This Sicilian ice-cream store is *the* place to have a *granita* (ice slush) in Florence; or try the *cremolata*, made from fruit pulp, including melon and blackberry.

🔳 G4 ✉ Via Ricasoli 60r ☎ 055 289 476 🕐 Daily 10am–midnight 🚌 C1, C2

ITALIAN CAKES

There are three main types of Tuscan cake. *Brioche* (breakfast pastries) are made with sweet yeast dough and come plain or filled with jam or custard. *Torte* (cakes) tend to be tarts, such as the ubiquitous *torta della nonna* (grandma's cake), a kind of custard tart, or *torta di ricotta*, in which ricotta is mixed with sugar and candied peel. Then there are all kinds of little cookies, most of which contain nuts and have names like *brutti ma buoni* (ugly but good).

LA GIOSTRA (€€€)

ristorantelagiostra.com

Prepare to be spoiled at this enclave of fine dining, owned by the children of a Hapsburg prince with a passion for food. Chef Ubaldo Tornarelli uses Tuscan specialities and seasonal ingredients for both traditional dishes and something more modern. Food and wines are impeccably sourced.

➕ G5 ✉ Borgo Pinti 12r ☎ 055 241 341 🕓 Mon–Fri 12.30–2.30, 7–late, Sat–Sun 7–late 🚌 C1, C2

LA MÉNAGÈRE (€€–€€€)

lamenagere.it

A café, homeware shop, cocktail bar and restaurant all under the same roof, retro, shabby-chic Ménagère is one of Florence's fashionable dining venues. The food is pan-Mediterranean with the odd creative twist.

➕ F4 ✉ Via de' Ginori 8r ☎ 055 075 0600 🕓 Daily 7am–2am 🚌 C1

LE MOSSACCE (€–€€)

trattorialemossacce.it

A bustling eatery between the Duomo and the Bargello, Le Mossacce serves excellent Tuscan food, including rich *zuppa Lombarda* soup with beans.

➕ G6 ✉ Via del Proconsolo 55r ☎ 055 294 361 🕓 Mon–Fri noon–2.30, 7–9.30 🚌 C1, C2

LORENZO NIGRO—IL LAMPREDOTTO (€)

This colourful food stall has been serving up cheap, rustic food to market workers since 1872. The speciality is *lampredotto* (cow's intestines) served in a bun with bright green salsa verde, but they also offer pasta and roast meats.

➕ F4 ✉ Mercato Centrale, Via del Ariento 🕓 Mon–Sat 7am–2pm 🚌 C1

ROBIGLIO (€€)

Old-fashioned Florentine bar/*pasticceria* par excellence, Robiglio's pastries are to die for. There is another branch in Via dei Servi.

➕ F5 ✉ Via dei Medici 16 ☎ 055 215 013 🕓 Daily 8am–8.30pm 🚌 C1

RUTH'S (€)

kosheruth.com

This bright, modern Jewish restaurant next to the synagogue serves an interesting mix of vegetarian (and fish), Middle Eastern and kosher food.

➕ H5 ✉ Via Farini 2a ☎ 055 248 0888 🕓 Sun–Thu 12.30–2.30, 7.30–1, Fri 12.30–2.30 🚌 C2, C3

SABATINI (€€€)

sabatinifirenze.it

This elegant, wood-panelled restaurant is a respected Florentine stalwart and particularly good for local steak and seafood risotto.

➕ E5 ✉ Via dei Panzani 9a 🕓 Tue–Sun 12.30–2.30, 7.30–10.30 🚌 C2

SERGIO GOZZI (€)

This no-frills, lunch-only trattoria by the side of San Lorenzo church has a daily-changing menu of excellent home-cooked Florentine specialities.

➕ F5 ✉ Piazza San Lorenzo 8r ☎ 055 281 941 🕓 Mon–Sat noon–3 🚌 C2, D

ZÀ-ZÀ (€)

trattoriazaza.it

The rustic Tuscan food at this charmingly old-fashioned, inexpensive trattoria near the Mercato Centrale is excellent. Popular with visitors, the inviting stone-walled interior is especially appealing in the summer heat.

➕ F4 ✉ Piazza del Mercato Centrale 26r ☎ 055 215 411 🕓 Daily 11–11 🚌 C2

Oltrarno

Literally translated as "beyond the Arno," the Oltrarno is the site of the Pitti Palace and the Boboli Gardens. It is also the most relaxed part of the city, least touched by tourism and with some of the best views.

Top 25

4

5

6

Piazza
di Cestello

✝ San Frediano
in Cestello

Piazza
N Sauro

LUNGARNO SODERINI

BORGO SAN FREDIANO

LUNGARNO GUICCIARDINI

Palazzo
Guicciardini

Piazza
Guicciardini

Palazzo
Frescobaldi

Piazza
del
Carmine

Piazza del
Carmine

Borgo d'Stella

**SANTO
SPIRITO**

Piazza
Frescobaldi

**Cappella
Brancacci**

Santa Maria
del Carmine

**Santo
Spirito**

Spirito

Palazzo
Firidolfi

Borgo San Jacopo

Piazza
di Santa
Felicita

Piazza
d'Rossi

Piazza di
Santa Maria
Soprarno

7

*Giardino
Torrigiani*

Piazza
S Spirito

Palazzo
Corsini

Palazzo
de' Pitti

Piazza
Romana

Palazzo
Pitti

Palazzo
Torrigiani

Piazza
S Felice

**Galleria d'Arte
Moderna**

**Santa
Felicita**

San
Girolamo

**Santo
Spirito**

**Museo della
Specola**

**Galleria del
Costume**

8

Giardino

**Museo delle
Porcellane**

Forte
del Nettuno

**Forte di
Belvedere**

Port
San

di Boboli

Porta
Romana

Piazzale di
Porta Romana

Istituto
d'Arte

Via d'Madonna
della Pace

BOBOLINO

S Leon
in Arc

VIALE NICCOLÒ MACHIAVELLI

9

0   250 m

0   250 yds

C   **D**   **E**   **F**

Cappella Brancacci

The frescoes in this tiny side chapel mark a watershed in the development of western art, when the painter Masaccio rediscovered the techniques for expressing emotions and thus paved the way for the Renaissance artists.

Miniature gem This small chapel is reached via the cloisters of the otherwise rather dull Santa Maria del Carmine. Two tiers of frescoes, commissioned in 1424 by wealthy merchant Felice Brancacci, illustrate the life of St. Peter, shown in his orange gown. The frescoes were designed by Masolino da Panicale, who began painting them with his brilliant pupil, Masaccio. In 1428 Masaccio took over from Masolino but died that year, aged 27; the rest of the frescoes were completed in the 1480s by Filippino Lippi.

OLTRARNO TOP 25

Restoration revelations In the 1980s the chapel was restored, with the removal of accumulated candle soot and layers of an 18th-century egg-based gum (which had formed a mould). The frescoes now have an intense radiance that makes it possible to see very clearly the shifts in emphasis between Masolino's work and that of Masaccio; contrast the serenity of Masolino's *Temptation of Adam and Eve,* with its soft colours and graceful figures, with the grief-stricken pair in Masaccio's *Expulsion of Adam and Eve from Paradise.* The restoration also highlighted Masaccio's mastery of chiaroscuro (light and shade), which, together with his grasp of perspective and ability to create amazingly life-like figures, set him apart from his contemporaries, many of whom deliberately copied his style.

THE BASICS

museicivicifiorentini.
comune.fi.it

➕ D6

✉ Santa Maria del
Carmine, Piazza del
Carmine (enter through
the cloisters)

☎ 055 276 8558; 055
276 8224 (advance reservations mandatory)

🕐 Mon, Wed–Sat 10–5,
Sun 1–5. Entrance by
reservation only

🚌 6, D

♿ Poor

✋ Moderate

Giardino di Boboli

Sculpture in the Boboli Gardens (left); pond and Isolotto (right)

THE BASICS

uffizi.it

➕ E8

✉ Piazza Pitti

☎ 055 238 8786

🕐 Jun–Aug daily 8.15–7.30; Apr–May, Sep daily 8.15–6.30; Mar, Oct daily 8.15–5.30; Nov–Feb daily 8.15–4.30; closed 1st and last Mon of month

🚇 D

♿ Good; some steps

💶 Garden inexpensive; combined ticket with Palazzo Pitti expensive

HIGHLIGHTS

● Bacchus fountain (1560)
● La Grotta Grande, a Mannerist cave-cum-sculpture gallery (1583–88)
● Views of the hills from the Giardino dei Cavallieri
● Limonaia (1785)—protected trees from the frost; now a huge garden shed
● The Isolotto

The Boboli Gardens are, quite literally, a breath of fresh air. They are the only easily accessible reservoir of greenery in central Florence, and a lovely retreat after a hard day's sightseeing.

Renaissance origins The Boboli Gardens were created for the Medici when they moved to the Palazzo Pitti in 1550. They represent a superb example of Italian Renaissance gardening, an interplay between nature and artifice expressed in a geometric arrangement of fountains, grass and low box hedges. In 1766 they were opened to the public, and in 1992 an entrance charge was imposed.

Amphitheatre Just behind the Palazzo Pitti is the amphitheatre, built where the stone for the palazzo was quarried. It was the site of the first-ever opera performance and is surrounded by mazelike alleys of fragrant, dusty bay trees. Go uphill past the Neptune Fountain (1565–68) to reach the Giardino dei Cavallieri, where roses and peonies wilt in the summer sun. The pretty building nearby houses the Museo delle Porcellane (Porcelain Museum, ▷ 86).

More to see The Viottolone, an avenue of cypresses planted in 1637 and studded with classical statues, leads to the Isolotto, an island set in a murky green pond dotted with crumbling statues. In the middle is a copy of Giambologna's *Oceanus* fountain (1576), the original of which is in the Bargello (▷ 24–25).

The Four Evangelists on the sacristy ceiling (left); Romanesque facade (right)

Standing on a hill to the south of Florence, San Miniato is a wonderful sight, its marble facade glistening in the sunlight. Close up it is even more appealing—a jewel of the Romanesque.

Christian martyr San Miniato (St. Minias) came to Florence from the Levant in the third century and was martyred in the Roman amphitheatre that stood on the site of Piazza della Signoria, by order of the Emperor Decius. It is said that his decapitated body picked up his head and walked into the hills. His shrine, the site of the present church, was built where he finally collapsed. The church was initially run by Benedictine monks, then by Cluniacs, and finally, from 1373 to now, by the Olivetans. In the Benedictine shop, on the right as you exit, monks sell honey and herbal potions.

An eagle visitation The church was built in 1018, with a green-and-white marble facade added at the end of the 11th century and mosaics in the 13th. On the pinnacle, a gilded copper statue of an eagle carries a bale of cloth: this is the symbol of the Arte di Calimala, the wool importers' guild, which supported the church in the Middle Ages.

Miraculous crucifix Inside, an inlaid floor (c.1207) incorporates zodiac and animal themes. In the nave is a chapel (1448) by Michelozzo, built to house a miraculous crucifix that is now in Santa Trinita.

THE BASICS

sanminiatoalmonte.it

🕂 H9

✉ Via Monte alle Croce, off Viale Galileo Galilei

☎ 055 234 2731

🕐 Mon–Sat 9.30–1, 3–7, Sun 8.15–7

🚌 12, 13

♿ Poor (make inquiries)

🎟 Free

HIGHLIGHTS

● Marble facade
● Inlaid floor
● Mosaics in the apse
● Cappella del Crocifisso
● Wooden ceiling
● Cardinal of Portugal Chapel (1473)

OLTRARNO TOP 25

Palazzo Pitti

HIGHLIGHTS

● Frescoed ceilings by
Pietro da Cortona, Galleria
Palatina
● Raphael's *Madonna of
the Chair* (c.1516)
● Titian's overtly sexual
Mary Magdalene (c.1531)
● Van Dyck's *Charles I and
Henrietta Maria* (c.1632)
● Titian's *Portrait of a
Gentleman* (1540)

TIPS

● It makes sense to con-
centrate on the Galleria
Palatina before moving on
to another gallery.
● Be prepared for crowds,
and sections to be closed.
● Book ahead.
● Leave time to relax after-
wards in the Giardino di
Boboli (▷ 82). Combined
tickets can be bought.

**The Pitti Palace, with its eight museums
and galleries, is unremittingly opulent,
an architectural complex celebrating
the power and wealth of the Medici,
Florence's ruling family.**

The building The wealthy banker Luca Pitti, a
business rival of the Medici, commissioned
architect Filippo Brunelleschi to design a vast
palazzo for his family in 1457. A century later,
the Pitti coffers were empty and the palace,
ironically, was purchased by Eleonora de'
Medici; her family filled the palace with their art
collections over the next few centuries.

The paintings The Galleria Palatina houses the
picture collection, comprising works just as
important as those in the Uffizi and still hung in

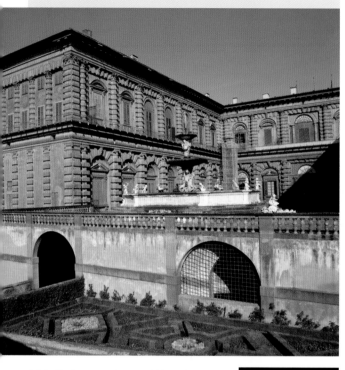

OLTRARNO TOP 25

tightly filled tiers, as they would have been in the 18th century. Masterpieces hang casually side by side with less important works, and some paintings are difficult to see. Amidst the jumble, you'll find major works by Filippo Lippi and Raphael, two superb paintings by Titian and a dramatic Caravaggio.

Other collections The Galleria leads to the stunningly extravagant and beautifully restored Appartamenti Reali (State Rooms), a chain of interconnecting rooms running along one side of the palazzo. These are followed by the Museo degli Argenti (Silver Museum), with a collection of luxury items that are often a triumph of wealth over good taste. Elsewhere, you'll find the Galleria del Costume (▷ 86) and the Galleria d'Arte Moderna (▷ 86).

THE BASICS

uffizi.it

🔢 E7

✉ Piazza Pitti

☎ Reservations 055 294 833

🕐 Tue–Sun 8.15–6.50. Argenti (▷ 82; same as Giardino di Boboli)

🚌 D

♿ Good

🎫 Galleria Palatina, Royal Apartments expensive; Galleria d'Arte Moderna combined ticket expensive; Museo degli Argenti (▷ 82, Boboli Gardens)

More to See

FORTE DI BELVEDERE

museicivicifiorentini.comune.fi.it

This imposing fortress was built by the Medici in 1590 as a refuge for the Grand Dukes in their struggle against the Florentine Republic, and a reminder of Medici military might.
➕ F8 ✉ Via San Leonardo ☎ 055 262 5962 ⏰ Jun–Sep for temporary exhibitions 🚍 D, plus walk 🎟 Free

GALLERIA D'ARTE MODERNA

uffizi.it

More than 30 rooms of paintings here span the mid-18th to mid-20th centuries. It is located in the main building of the Palazzo Pitti on the floor above the Palatina.
➕ E7 ✉ Palazzo Pitti, Piazza Pitti ☎ 055 238 8616 ⏰ Tue–Sun 8.15–6.50 🚍 D 🦽 Good 🎟 Inclusive ticket with Galleria Palatina (▷ 84) expensive

GALLERIA DEL COSTUME

uffizi.it

In the Palazzina Meridiana in the south wing of the Pitti, this is one for devotees of clothes and fashion. The collection illustrates the history of costume from the 18th century up until the 1920s.
➕ E7 ✉ Palazzo Pitti, Piazza Pitti ☎ 055 238 8614 ⏰ Giardino di Boboli (▷ 82, panel) 🚍 D 🦽 Good 🎟 Inclusive ticket with Museo degli Argenti, Museo delle Porcellane, Giardino di Boboli expensive

MUSEO DELLE PORCELLANE

uffizi.it

French, Italian, German and Viennese porcelain and ceramics are all housed in a pavilion at the top of the Giardino di Boboli.
➕ E8 ✉ Giardino di Boboli, Piazza Pitti ☎ 055 238 8709 ⏰ Giardino di Boboli (▷ 82, panel) 🚍 D 🦽 Good, some steps 🎟 Inclusive ticket with Museo degli Argenti, Galleria del Costume and Giardino di Boboli expensive

MUSEO DELLA SPECOLA

msn.unifi.it

"La Specola" is so called after the observatory that used to be here. This museum of zoology and natural history is part of the university.

View from Piazzale Michelangelo

An unusual highlight is the Cere Anatomiche, a gruesome set of 18th-century wax models of bits of human bodies.

🔲 E7 ✉ Via Romana 17 ☎ 055 228 8251 ⏰ Jun–Sep Tue–Sun 10.30–5.30; Oct–May Tue–Sun 9.30–4.30 🚌 11, D ♿ Good 💶 Expensive

PIAZZALE MICHELANGELO

Despite the fact that Piazzale Michelangelo is frequented by busloads of tourists, this stupendous vantage point is still very much worth the trip. Ignore the poor green copy of Michelangelo's *David* and the souvenir stalls, beware of pickpockets and soak up the view.

🔲 H8 ✉ Viale Galileo Galilei 🚌 12, 13 ♿ Good 💶 Free

PONTE ALLE GRAZIE

Dating from 1237, when it was known as Ponte Rubaconte (after the chief magistrate who commissioned it), the bridge was rebuilt to its 18th-century design after World War II. Its present name is from the oratory of Santa Maria delle Grazie, which once stood here.

🔲 G7 🔲 C3, D, 6

SANTA FELICITA

This second-century church is the second-oldest in Florence, after San Lorenzo. The highlight is Pontormo's Mannerist *Deposition* (1525–28) in the Cappella Caponi: a stunning vortex of contorted forms in vibrant shades of pink, blue and green.

🔲 F7 ✉ Piazza Santa Felicita ⏰ 055 213 018 ⏰ Mon–Sat 9–12, 3.30–5.30; closed during services. Mass: Sun 9, 11, Mon–Sat 6pm 🚌 D ♿ Poor 💶 Free

SANTO SPIRITO

basilicasantospirito.it

Designed by Filippo Brunelleschi in 1435, this church has an unfinished 18th-century baroque facade. The *cenacolo* (refectory) houses a fresco of the *Last Supper* by Nardo di Cione.

🔲 E7 ✉ Piazza Santo Spirito ☎ 055 210 030 ⏰ Thu–Tue 10–12.30, 4–5.30; closed during services 🚌 D ♿ Poor 💶 Free

Santo Spirito

Around the Oltrarno

This walk begins amid the bustle of the Oltrarno, yet soon passes through more tranquil surroundings to catch a glimpse of local life.

DISTANCE: 2km (1 mile) **ALLOW:** 2–3 hours

START

PONTE VECCHIO (▷ 34–35)
🔲 F7 🚌 C3

END

PIAZZALE MICHELANGELO (▷ 87)
🔲 H8 🚌 12, 13

① In summer this walk can be baking hot; start early in the morning or after 4pm and take a bottle of water. Plan a midday picnic at the Forte di Belvedere (▷ 86).

② Set off from the south side of the Ponte Vecchio in Oltrarno. With your back to the bridge, take the first square on your left, Piazza di Santa Felicita.

③ Here you will find Pontormo's *Deposition* in Santa Felicita (▷ 87) church. Take the road on the left of the church, the Costa di San Giorgio, where Galileo lived at No. 19.

④ Continue up its steep slope. At the top, you pass through Porta di San Giorgio (1260), the oldest city gate, with a carving of St. George slaying the dragon.

⑧ Continue downhill to Piazzale Michelangelo for great views. A No. 12 bus will take you back down to Ponte alle Grazie (▷ 87).

⑦ A little way up take the steep Via di San Salvadore al Monte on the left, which crosses Viale Galileo Galilei. Climb the hill flanked by cypress trees that continues up toward San Miniato (▷ 83). Return to Viale Galileo Galilei and go right.

⑥ After the entrance to Forte di Belvedere, descend steeply along the 13th-century defensive city walls. At the bottom of the hill, by the small gateway of Porta San Miniato, turn right and head up Via del Monte alle Croci.

⑤ Follow Via del Belvedere, and leave the 1590 Forte di Belvedere on your right.

Shopping

ANNA
annapitti.it
This shop is in a 300-year-old tower in front of the Pitti Palace. Anna sells a great range of leather goods, knitwear, scarves and ties for men and women.
🔳 E7 ✉ Piazza Pitti 38–40r ☎ 055 283 787 📠 D

ANTICO SETIFICIO FIORENTINO
anticosetificiofiorentino.com
Only if you fix up an appointment in advance can you visit this old Florentine silk factory that provides fabric for some of Italy's most sought-after designers. Much of the fabric is woven using traditional methods and 18th-century looms.
🔳 C6 ✉ Via Lorenzo Bartolini 4 ☎ 055 213 861 📠 D

BARTOLOZZI & MAIOLI
bartolozziemaioli.it
This antiques shop gives an insight into the Florentine love of ostentatious adornment. The quality is excellent but pieces are expensive.
🔳 E7 ✉ Via Vellutini 5r ☎ 055 281 723 📠 D

BOTTEGA DELLE STAMPE
bottegadellestampe.com
Framed and unframed antique or art nouveau prints (known in Italy as Liberty) are on sale in this elegant store.
🔳 E6 ✉ Borgo San Jacopo 56r ☎ 055 295 396 📠 D

LA CASA DELLA STAMPA
Vivianna is a lithographer who hand-tints many of these beautiful prints. There is a huge selection of Florentine scenes from the Medici era and painted studies of butterflies and plants.
🔳 E7 ✉ Sdrucciolo de Pitti 11r ☎ 055 285 755 📠 D

ENOTECA PERI
A no-nonsense wine and oil shop selling good-quality regional products, this *enoteca* lies just over the Santa Trinita bridge.
🔳 E7 ✉ Via Maggio 5r ☎ 055 212 674 📠 D

GIULIO GIANNINI E FIGLIO
giuliogiannini.it
The best known of Florence's stationery shops, established in 1856, sells tasteful cards and books bound in leather, as well as beautifully finished desktop paraphernalia, letter racks and pen holders, all covered with marbled paper.
🔳 E7 ✉ Piazza Pitti 37r ☎ 055 212 621 📠 D

J. T. CASINI
jennifertattanelli.it
The latest in Italian and international designer clothing for women is on sale here. Up-and-coming designers are showcased alongside well-known brands.
🔳 E7 ✉ Piazza Pitti 30–31r ☎ 055 219 324 📠 D

POTTERY FACTS

Traditional Italian ceramics are known as majolica, terracotta covered with a brilliant tin-based glaze. Arabic ceramics inspired pots made for the Medici court at Montelupo, to the west of Florence. Deruta in Umbria makes flowery designs in blue on white or yellow. Designs in turquoise on white are also much in evidence. Tuscan peasant wares, white or yellow, splashed with green or blue spots, are increasingly popular. Among the best-known classic designs is Gran Faenza, with green, red and blue floral designs on a pale grey-blue background. Most shops offer shipping.

MADOVA GLOVES

madova.com

This family-run business, with its factory at the back of the shop, was established in 1919 and sells fine gloves lined with silk, cashmere and fur in every hue.

➕ E7 ✉ Via Guicciardini 1r ☎ 055 239 6526 🚌 D

MOLERIA LOCCHI

locchi.com

This shop, deep in the southern reaches of the Oltrarno, sells the most extraordinary glass you will see outside Venice, created using traditional methods.

➕ C7 ✉ Via Domenico Burchiello 10 ☎ 055 229 8371 🚌 D, 12, 13

OLIO & CONVIVIUM

oliorestaurant.it

This pristine delicatessen has beautiful displays of charcuterie, bakery goods, cheeses, and a huge range of olive oils and wine. There's an adjoining restaurant.

➕ E6 ✉ Via Santo Spirito 4 ☎ 055 265 8198 🚌 D, 11

RIVE GAUCHE

rivegaucheshoes.com

Many people visit Florence to buy the leather goods for which the city is renowned, in particular shoes. This shop takes you back in time with its beautiful handmade shoes and boots.

➕ E7 ✉ Via Guicciardini 31r ☎ 055 213 474 🚌 D

SARA AMRHEIN

sara-amrhein.com

Vibrant colour and exquisite detailing are the hallmarks of Sara's quirky jewellery, where clay is moulded into mainly flower and petal shapes to produce necklaces and earrings.

➕ E7 ✉ Via dello Sprone 9–11r 🚌 D

ARTISANS

The district of Oltrarno is characterized by small artisan workshops producing leather goods, textiles, ceramics, paper products and jewellery. Many of these businesses have been in the same family for generations and extreme skill and passion is employed in the workmanship.

SFORNO

ilsantobevitore.com

Rather than the usual Italian-style goods, Sforno makes mouthwatering brownies, cheesecake, frangipane tarts, savoury quiches and a whole range of different pizzas by the slice. At lunchtime there are also salads and soups to eat in or take away.

➕ D7 ✉ Via Santa Monaca 3r ☎ 055 239 8580 🚌 C3, D

STEFANO BEMER

stefanobemer.it

For exquisitely made men's shoes, head to this ex-chapel in San Niccolò, where you'll find Oxfords, Derbys, monkstraps, moccasins—bespoke or ready to wear—plus elegant belts, wallets and watch straps. Prices are high but the shoes will last a lifetime.

➕ H7 ✉ Via San Niccolò 2 ☎ 055 046 0476 🚌 C3, D

IL TORCHIO

legatoriailtorchio.com

As you walk into this stationery shop you are instantly aware that this is a place where things are made, not just a showroom. You can buy sheets of marbled paper or have it made up to suit your requirements. There are also ready-made marbled paper goods available.

➕ F7 ✉ Via dei Bardi 17 ☎ 055 234 2862 🚌 C, D

Entertainment and Nightlife

LA CITÉ

Come here in the day to sample a welcoming French-style literary café or, better still, in the evening, when the space becomes a fashionable music venue, with live acts and good cocktails.
🔼 D6 ⊠ Borgo San Frediano 8 ☎ 349 901 1105 🚌 D, 6

NOF CLUB

nofclub.it
There's live music six nights a week from 10.30 till around 2am at this great little club, tucked away behind a low-key door. Excellent drink and a friendly vibe attract the crowds.
🔼 D6 ⊠ Borgo San Frediano 17r ☎ 333 614 5376 🚌 D, 6

UNIVERSALE

universalefirenze.it
This former cinema space is now dedicated to dance music, cocktail drinking

and Italian food. The music is house during the week and more eclectic on Saturday, with funk, jazz and exotica.
🔼 C6 ⊠ Via Pisana 77r ☎ 055 221 122 🕙 Closed Mon, Tue, Wed 🚌 6, 12

VOLUME

This popular retro-chic Oltrarno haunt on lovely Piazza Santo Spirito is open all day, but things really get lively at aperitivo time, when the music cranks up and punters spill onto the terrace.
🔼 E7 ⊠ Piazza Santo Spirito 5r ☎ 055 238 1460 🚌 C3, D, 6, 11

Where to Eat

AL TRANVAI (€)

altranvai.it
Diners pack into this lively trattoria on a quiet neighbourhood square in the Oltrarno. Popular (with locals) is *frattaglie* (a mind-boggling range of offal) but the menu changes every day.

🔼 C7 ⊠ Piazza Torquato Tasso 14r ☎ 055 225 197 🕙 Tue–Sat 12.15–3, 7–10.45, Mon 7–10.45 🚌 12, 13

BURRO E ACCIUGHE (€€)

burroeacciughe.com
Butter and Anchovies is a retro-rustic restaurant specializing in fish and seafood dishes. Expect marinated salmon, tagliatelle with sea bream and rocket and olive pesto, and grilled tuna steak, plus a good selection of wines.
🔼 C6 ⊠ Via dell'Orto 35r ☎ 055 045 7286 🕙 Tue–Fri 7.30pm–midnight, Sat–Sun 12.30–2.30, 7.30–midnight 🚌 D, 6

CAMMILLO (€€–€€€)

The Masiero family's long-established trattoria attracts a fashionable crowd and Italian celebrities, enticed by the home-made pasta, *baccalà* (salted cod) dishes and expertly cooked meats. Try some of the house virgin olive oil with bread.

🔲 E6 ⊠ Borgo San Jacopo 57r ☎ 055 212 427 ⏱ Thu–Mon noon–2.30, 7.30–10.30 🚍 D

LA CASALINGA (€–€€)

trattorialacasalinga.it

A busy and down-to-earth family-run trattoria serving rustic Florentine fare, this is a good place to try *bollito* (boiled meat) and *ribollita*, the Florentine soup made with bread and vegetables.

🔲 B8 ⊠ Via dei Michelozzi 9r ☎ 055 218 624 ⏱ Mon–Sat noon–2.30, 7–10 🚍 D

DEL CARMINE (€–€€)

With its pleasant terrace and daily specials, this traditional neighbourhood trattoria is popular with both locals and visitors. Try the *tagliata*—sliced grilled steak topped with rocket and parmesan.

CONTRADICTION

The concept of vegetarianism is not one that sits easily with Italian ideas about food, and there are very few vegetarian restaurants in Italy. However, there are few better countries for those who do not eat meat (or fish). Many pasta dishes contain no meat—pesto, tomato sauce or ravioli stuffed with spinach and ricotta, to name but a few. For a main course, try *grigliata di verdura* (grilled vegetables) or restaurant staples such as *parmigiana di melanzane* (aubergine layered with tomato and mozzarella, and baked with a Parmesan crust), *mozzarella in carrozza* (fried mozzarella) and *frittate* (omelettes).

🔲 D6 ⊠ Piazza del Carmine 18r ☎ 055 218 601 ⏱ Mon–Sat 12.15–2.30, 7.15–10.30 🚍 C3, D, 6

OLIVIA (€)

oliviafirenze.com

To taste Tuscany's "liquid gold" (extra virgin olive oil), try this bright little shop-cum-restaurant that sells all things olive oil related. Everything on the menu is prepared with lashings of extra virgin, even the ice cream.

🔲 E7 ⊠ Piazza Pitti 14r ☎ 055 267 0359 ⏱ Mon–Wed, Sun noon–5, Fri–Sat noon–10 🚍 C3, D

IL SANTO BEVITORE (€€)

ilsantobevitore.com

Offering a creative take on Tuscan and Italian classics, Santo Bevitore has long been one of Florence's most fashionable restaurants.

🔲 D6 ⊠ Via Santo Spirito 64–66r ☎ 055 211 264 ⏱ Mon 7.30–11pm, Tue–Sun 12.30–2.30, 7.30–11 🚍 C3, D, 6, 11

SANTO SPIRITO (€–€€)

osteriasantospirito.it

This charming trattoria has outdoor seating and a menu of robust main courses, such as oven-baked gnocchi in cheese and flavoured with truffles. It's good for vegetarians and great for kids.

🔲 E7 ⊠ Piazza Santo Spirito 16r ☎ 055 238 2383 ⏱ Daily 11–11 🚍 D, 11

LE VOLPI E L'UVA (€)

levolpieluva.com

The Foxes and Grapes is a delightful little wine bar tucked away behind the Ponte Vecchio where you can wash down pungent Italian salamis and cheeses with wines from all over Italy.

🔲 F7 ⊠ Piazza dei Rossi 1r ☎ 055 239 8132 ⏱ Mon–Sat 11–9 🚍 C3, D

Farther Afield

There is plenty to do to escape the crowds or to have a change of scenery. Choose from pretty Fiesole, only 7km (4 miles) away; medieval gems such as Siena, Lucca and San Gimignano; Pisa, with its irresistible Leaning Tower; or the enchanting wine region of Chianti.

FARTHER AFIELD TOP 25

Tuscan countryside (left); Fiesole's amphitheatre (below) and bell tower (right)

Fiesole

Perched on a hillside 7km (4 miles) above Florence, this delightful Etruscan-Roman town offers outstanding views over the city and the chance to visit an impressive archaeological complex, complete with amphitheatre, baths and a temple.

Take a stroll Fiesole is the perfect antidote to hectic sightseeing in central Florence, while the bus ride there, climbing the winding road, is a pleasing introduction to the Tuscan countryside. Head first to the tourist information office to pick up a town map, which includes three walking routes that take in the best views.

The archaeological area The entrance ticket to Fiesole's important Roman and Etruscan remains includes the Museo Civico and the small Museo Bandini. Set high up on a hillside, the open-air site features an Etruscan temple, the superbly preserved first-century AD Roman amphitheatre and the partially restored Roman baths. The theatre, holding 3,000 people, is still used today for performances and concerts during the Fiesole Summer Festival (▷ 105). On Via Dupré, Museo Bandini houses 13th- to 15th-century Florentine paintings and Luca della Robbia terracottas.

Around the town Landmarks include the Duomo, with its 13th-century bell tower, and the striking 14th-century Palazzo Communale, now occupied by the town council. Traditional restaurants and cafés overlook the main square.

THE BASICS

museidifiesole.it
+ See map ▷ 95
⊠ Via Portigiani 1
☎ 055 596 1293
🕐 Archaeological area and museum Apr–Sep daily 10–7; Nov–Feb Wed–Mon 10–3; Mar, Oct daily 10–6. Museo Bandini Apr–Sep Fri–Sun 9–7; Mar, Oct Fri–Sun 10–6; Nov–Feb Fri–Sun 9–3
🚌 7
♿ Good
💷 Combined ticket expensive

HIGHLIGHTS

● Views over Florence
● Archaeological area
● Roman amphitheatre
● Walks in the Tuscan countryside

More to See

LE CASCINE

Once the site of the Medici dairy farms (*cascine*), Florence's largest park is a 20- to 30-minute walk west of the city centre. It has an open-air swimming pool and a market every Tuesday. The area can be rather seedy by night.

➕ A3 ⊠ Ponte della Vittoria ⏰ Daily 24 hours 🚌 17, 18 ⚿ Good 💶 Free

CERTOSA DEL GALLUZZO

certosadifirenze.it

This great Carthusian monastery was once occupied by 18 monks, who lived silent lives. The stunning Chiostro Grande is decorated with *tondi* (circular works of art) by Andrea and Giovanni della Robbia. The visit includes the Palazzo degli Studi, which holds the *Scenes from the Passion* frescoes executed by Pontormo while he was sheltered here during the 1522 plague.

➕ See map ▷ 94 ⊠ Via della Certosa 1 ☎ 055 204 9226 ⏰ Tours only: Apr–Sep Tue–Sat 10, 11, 3, 4, 5, Sun 3, 4, 5; Oct–Mar no 5pm tour 🚌 37 ⚿ Good 💶 Donation

FORTEZZA DA BASSO

An enormous defensive fortress built in 1534 by Antonio da Sangallo il Giovane to the orders of Alessandro de' Medici, this citadel now hosts trade fairs, exhibitions and other events while cars and buses hurtle past on all sides.

➕ E3 ⊠ Viale Filippo Strozzi ☎ Contact tourist office for events 🚌 4, 12, 13, 14, 20, 23

MUSEO STIBBERT

museostibbert.it

This bizarre museum, with its superb armour collection, makes a fascinating diversion. The collection was amassed by Frederick Stibbert (1838–1906), who travelled the world, purchasing armour, porcelain, paintings, costumes and much more. The museum is set in pleasant wooded grounds, complete with an Egyptian-style folly.

➕ See map ▷ 94 ⊠ Via Frederico Stibbert 26 ☎ 055 486 049 ⏰ Mon–Wed 10–2, Fri–Sun 10–6 🚌 4 to Via Vittorio Emanuele II and steep walk to museum ⚿ Access to most parts 💶 Moderate ❓ Café, bookshop

Altar in the 14th-century Certosa del Galluzzo

Excursions

CHIANTI

The name Chianti, familiar to wine lovers everywhere, is given to the beautiful, hilly region between Florence and Siena, where dense woods are punctuated by farms, villas, vineyards and olive groves, and dotted with appealing small towns.

This is an area best explored by car, as public transport is sporadic and limited. It's traversed by a designated wine route, the Strada Chiantigiana (SS222), which winds its way through the heart of the district. It's twisting and thickly wooded, so you'll want to make frequent stops, both in the little towns such as Greve, Radda, Gaiole and Castellina and perhaps to visit the vineyards along its route.

Heading south from Florence, make your first stop at Greve in Chianti, whose triangular main square, Piazza Matteotti, is lined with arcaded buildings, many occupied by wine shops. Look out for the statue of local hero Giovanni Verrazzano, who in 1524 was the first European to enter New York harbour. South again from here, you'll come to Radda in Chianti, a hilltop town with superb views, centred around the Palazzo Comunale, decorated with the coats of arm of its important families; this was for centuries the headquarters of the Chianti League. Opposite is the church of San Niccolo, and the surrounding maze of streets is lined with gracious mansions dating from the 15th and 16th centuries.

Lying 6km (4 miles) further is the Badia a Coltibuono, an 11th-century abbey, now used for *agriturismo* (farm stays), with a superb Romanesque church, standing surrounded by one of Chianti's finest wine estates. From here, work your way east to Castellina in Chianti, a strategically situated town with solid walls and a big fortress (the Rocca). The archaeological museum here displays many interesting finds from this part of the region, especially Etruscan items from Montecalvario. The town is also an excellent place to buy wine and olive oil.

THE BASICS

terresiena.it
chianti.com
Distance: 42km (26 miles) to Castellina in Chianti
Journey Time: 45–60 minutes by car
🚹 Via Ferruccio 40, Castellina in Chianti; Piazza Castello 1, Radda in Chianti ☎ Castellina: 0577 741 392; Radda: 0577 738 494

FARTHER AFIELD EXCURSIONS

THE BASICS

turismo.lucca.it
Distance: 50km (31 miles)
Journey Time: About
1 hour
🚆 Regular departures
from Santa Maria Novella
station to Lucca Centrale
🛈 Porto San Donato,
Piazzale Verdi ☎ 0583
583 150 🕐 Apr–Oct daily
9.30–6.30; Nov–Mar daily
9.30–4.30
Villa Guinigi
luccamuseinazionali.it
✉ Via della Quarquonia
☎ 0583 496 033
🕐 Tue–Sat 9.30–7
Palazzo Mansi
luccasmuseinazionali.it
✉ Via Galli Tassi 43
☎ 0583 55570
🕐 Tue–Sat 9.30–7

LUCCA

Magnificent Renaissance walls, pierced by gateways, completely enclose the historic centre of Lucca, a prosperous and charming town that's home to a rich heritage of churches, palazzi and museums. Its cobbled streets provide some great shopping and markets, while its squares offer vibrant café life and excellent restaurants.

Arriving by train, head up Via Vittorio Emanuele to start your explorations in Piazza Napoleone. From here, it's a couple of minutes to the other central square, Piazza San Michele, and an easy stroll to all of Lucca's other main sights. Just off Napoleone, you'll find the Duomo, a stunning Romanesque cathedral, famous for its 11th- to 13th-century door reliefs. Across the square is San Giovanni e Reparata, near which you can pick up Via Fillungo (Long Thread Street), an elegant and tempting shopping street, which arrows through the town centre. En route, pause at the Pisa-Romanesque church of San Michele in Foro, with its glorious facade, which stands on what was the Roman forum.

Fillungo continues to the iconic Piazza Anfiteatro, occupying the space of the Roman amphitheatre that once stood here—you can still see traces of arches and columns embedded in the surrounding buildings. Nearby is the splendid church of San Frediano, crammed with 12th- and 13th-century sculpture, its facade glittering with mosaics. To the south of Anfiteatro you can climb the 238 steps to the top of the iconic Torre Guinigi, crowned by holm oaks. Museum lovers could head for Lucca's main museums, Villa Guinigi and Palazzo Mansi, or visit the house where the composer Puccini was born in Viale Puccini.

Do factor in time to walk or cycle along the tree-lined walls. Built between 1520 and 1650, they encircle the town for 4km (2.5 miles) and give spectacular views over towards the Apuan Alps, especially beautiful when snow-covered in winter.

PISA

A major medieval maritime power, Pisa today draws the crowds to the renowned Campo dei Miracoli, home to the iconic Leaning Tower. The city's many other pleasures include an evocative old quarter, piazzas, palaces and churches, some good shopping and a tranquil riverside location.

The Campo dei Miracoli (Field of Miracles) is a superb complex of Pisan-Romanesque architecture, comprising the Duomo (cathedral); the Battistero (baptistery), the largest in Italy and boasting extraordinary acoustics; and the famous campanile, the Torre Pendente (Leaning Tower), all set in a sweeping green space. All three buildings date from the 11th and 12th centuries and have similar decorative, and unifying, points—the grey and white marble, the niches and arcaded columns. The tower started leaning even before its completion in 1350, and was finally stabilized in the 1990s, to reopen in 2001; today visitors can climb the 251 uneven steps that wind up round the outside of the tower, but make sure to book ahead. The adjoining museum is packed with both information and treasures from down the centuries.

From here, Via Carducci and Borgo Stretto, lined with graceful, mainly Renaissance palaces, lead through the old city centre. Do detour west to Piazza dei Cavalieri, the heart of medieval Pisa, today lined with 16th-century palazzi decorated with *sgraffito*. The wonderfully vibrant daily food market takes place round here, and you'll emerge on to the Lungarni, the elegant, palace-lined streets that line the River Arno. This area is rich in churches and is home to Pisa's main museums, the Museo Nazionale di San Matteo and the Palazzo Reale, once a Medici residence. Also on the Lungarno is the lovely Pisan-Gothic Santa Maria della Spina (St. Mary of the Thorn), built in 1323 beside the river as an oratory for seamen and travellers, and moved in 1871 to escape flooding.

THE BASICS

turismo.pisa.it

Distance: 80km (50 miles)

Journey Time: About 1 hour

🚆 Frequent departures from Santa Maria Novella

🛈 Piazza Duomo 7 (Piazza dei Miracoli)

☎ 050 550 100 🕐 Mar–Oct daily 9.30–5.30; Nov–Feb daily 9–5

Campo dei Miracoli

opapisa.it

🕐 Daily 9–7. For Leaning Tower, timed tickets only; book online up to 20 days ahead

Museo Nazionale di San Matteo

polomusealetoscana.beniculturali.it

✉ Piazza San Matteo in Soarto 1

☎ 050 541 865

🕐 Tue–Sat 8.30–12.30, 2–6

Palazzo Reale

polomusealetoscana.beniculturali.it

✉ Lungarno Pacinotti 46

☎ 050 926 573

🕐 Wed–Mon 9–2

PISTOIA

East from Prato, at the foot of the Apennines, lies Pistoia, today the centre of a huge and renowned plant and flower industry. Try and visit on a Wednesday or Saturday when one of Italy's largest and best markets is held in the central Piazza del Duomo. This square is home to the 10th-century cathedral of San Zeno, with its eye-popping solid silver altar, and the adjoining octagonal baptistery. The piazza is also the site of the 14th-century Palazzo degli Anziani, home to Pistoia's Museo Civico, which has a lovely art collection with pieces from the Romanesque to the 19th century.

About 15 minutes' walk away is the Ospedale del Ceppo, a hospital founded in the 13th century, which has an attractive loggia decorated with a colourful frieze. You can't go inside but you can take a tour of the atmospheric underground cellar and tunnels.

PRATO

Visiting Prato, a prosperous and ancient town to the northeast of Florence, will give you an insight into modern Tuscany, with its high living standards and thriving economy—alongside the palazzi and artistic treasures from the past.

Prato has made its money from textiles since medieval times, when 13th-century merchants shipped their cloth all over Europe. It still manufactures on a large scale, as the outer sprawl of industry and clothing factory outlets testify. Inside the medieval walls, however, things are very different. The vast Castello dell'Imperatore was built by Frederick II between 1217 and 1248 and was later linked by an underground passage to the city walls. Nearby is the 12th-century Duomo, with its Renaissance sculpture and Filippo Lippi frescoes, while the church of Santa Maria delle Carceri, designed by Sangallo, is a Renaissance masterpiece.

Prato is also a food capital and the home of mortadella cured meat. Try it with the local bread, *bozza*, made in the traditional Tuscan way without salt.

THE BASICS

pistoiaturismo.it
Distance: 41km (26 miles)
Journey Time: 40 minutes
Frequent services from Santa Maria Novella
Piazza del Duomo 4
0573 21622 Daily 9–1, 3–5.30
Museo Civico
musei.comune.pistoia.it
Piazza Duomo 1
0573 371 296
Tue–Fri 10–4, Sat–Sun 10–6
Ospedale del Ceppo
Piazza Giovanni XXIII 13
0573 368 023
Tours daily 10.30–5

THE BASICS

pratoturismo.it
Distance: 20km (13 miles)
Journey Time: 20 minutes
Frequent services from Santa Maria Novella
Palazzo Pretorio, Piazza del Comune 0574 24112 Mon–Sat 9.30–7, Sun 9.30–6.30
Castello dell'Imperatore
Piazza Santa Maria delle Carceri 27
0574 38207
Apr–Sep daily 10–1, 3–7; Oct–Mar daily 10–4

SAN GIMIGNANO

San Gimignano, the quintessential medieval Tuscan village, surrounded by idyllic landscape, is dominated by a crop of towers that gives it one of the country's most evocative skylines. Within its walls are picture-perfect old streets lined with towers and palazzi, lovely squares, a superb Collegiata church, an excellent museum and shops and restaurants packed with temptations.

From the Porta San Giovanni, the south gate, Via San Giovanni leads uphill to the two interlocking squares that form the town's hub. The first, Piazza della Cisterna, is named for the octagonal 13th-century well in its centre, and leads through to Piazza del Duomo, dominated by the wonderfully frescoed church known as the Collegiata. Both squares are surrounded by palazzi and soaring towers, built by the town's constantly feuding leading families during the late 12th to mid-14th centuries. Today there 14 towers, all that remain of the original 72. The Black Death ended the town's prosperity and independence, and it became a rural backwater, subject to Florence. It was only post-World War II tourism and the revival of its winemaking industry that saw recovery.

West of the Piazza del Duomo looms the fortress of Montestaffoli, built in the 14th century to protect the town against the Sienese. It is now in ruins and only one of the turrets is open to visitors, but the views from here are superb.

Next to the Collegiata lies the Palazzo Comunale, home to a good museum and art gallery and giving access to the only tower you can climb. Outside again, Via San Matteo runs downhill to the northern gate and the great church of Sant'Agostino, home to a vibrant fresco cycle by Benozzo Gozzoli.

Leave time to explore the shops and sample some Vernaccia, the town's own white wine. Better still, spend a night, when you can experience the town at its best, when the huge crowds of day visitors have gone.

THE BASICS

sangimignano.com
Distance: 59km (36 miles)
Journey Time: 45–90 minutes by bus
🚌 From Florence to Siena; see tiemmespa.it for details
ℹ️ Piazza del Duomo 1 ☎ 0577 940 008
🕐 Mar–Oct daily 9–1, 3–6; Nov–Feb Mon–Sat 9–1, 2–4.30, Sun 10–4

Collegiata
duomosangimignano.it
✉️ Piazza del Duomo
☎ 0577 286 300
🕐 Apr–Oct Mon–Fri 10–7.30, Sat 10–5.30, Sun 12.30–7.30; Nov–Mar Mon–Sat 10–5, Sun 12.30–5

Palazzo Comunale
sangimignanomusei.it
✉️ Piazza del Duomo
☎ 0577 286 300
🕐 Apr–Sep daily 10–7.30; Oct–Mar daily 11–5.30

Sant'Agostino
✉️ Piazza Sant'Agostino
☎ 0577 907 012
🕐 Apr–Oct daily 7–12, 3–7; Nov–Mar daily 7–12, 3–6

THE BASICS

terresiena.it

Distance: 66km (41 miles)
Journey Time: 1–2 hours

🚆 Regular departures from Santa Maria Novella

🚌 SITA bus from Florence bus station

ℹ️ Santa Maria della Scala, Piazza del Duomo 1 ☎ 0577 280 551

🕐 Mon–Fri 10.30–4.30, Sat–Sun 10.30–6.30

Palazzo Pubblico

comune.siena.it

✉️ Piazza del Campo 1

☎ 0577 292 232

🕐 Mid-Mar to Oct daily 10–7; Nov to mid-Mar daily 10–6

Duomo

operaduomo.siena.it

✉️ Piazza del Duomo

☎ 0577 286 300

🕐 Mar–Nov daily 10.30–7; Dec–Feb daily 10.30–5.30

Santa Maria della Scala

santamariadellascala.com

✉️ Piazza del Duomo 2

☎ 0577 286 300

🕐 Mid-Mar to mid-Oct daily 10–7; mid-Oct to mid-Mar daily 1–5

Pinacoteca Nazionale

pinacotecanazionale.siena.it

✉️ Via San Pietro 29

☎ 0577 282 161

🕐 Tue–Sat 8.15–7.15, Sun–Mon 9–1

SIENA

One of the loveliest and best preserved of Italy's medieval cities, beautiful Siena offers a plethora of delights—a superb Duomo, a magnificent piazza, some fine civic buildings and museums, while its good restaurants, interesting shops and vibrant university and arts scene add to its charms.

Siena's focal point is the Campo, a huge, sloping, scallop-shaped open space at the heart of a mesh of cobbled streets and narrow stepped alleys. At the bottom stands the Palazzo Pubblico, the seat of government in the days of the Sienese republic, today housing an excellent museum in its frescoed rooms. Beside it soars the Torre della Mangia, the civic bell tower—climb its 388 steps for fabulous views out to the countryside.

Uphill from the Campo, the black-and-white-striped Gothic Duomo (cathedral) was built between 1136 and 1382, and its dim interior, with its superb marble mosaic floor, is studded with treasures, including Pisano's marble pulpit. Outside, next to the excellent cathedral museum, is a vast unfinished nave, begun in 1339 but abandoned during the Black Death of 1348, which ended Siena's prosperity. Don't miss the baptistery and crypt, or the vibrant Piccolomini Library, which is lined with frescoes by Pinturicchio and has an amazing colourful ceiling. There are more frescoes in Santa Maria della Scala, which stands opposite the Duomo and was once the city's hospital.

You could also visit the nearby Pinacoteca Nazionale, home to an outstanding collection of Sienese Gothic paintings.

Many tourists plan a visit to Siena to coincide with the Palio, a famous bareback horse race in the Campo held twice annually on 2 July and 16 August, and which featured in the James Bond movie *Quantum of Solace*. Tickets sell out months in advance so plan ahead if you want to witness this spectacle, and be prepared to stand for hours in dense crowds in the heat.

Entertainment and Nightlife

MAGGIO MUSICALE FIORENTINO

This major musical festival held in May and June includes opera and ballet as well as orchestral concerts and chamber music. It has its own orchestra and chorus. The main venue is the Opera di Firenze (▷ 74); the Teatro della Pergola (▷ 74) and the Teatro Verdi (▷ 46) are used for more intimate concerts. The main box office is at the Opera di Firenze.

AUDITORIUM FLOG

flog.it

This is probably the best known of Florence's live music venues, where music of all kinds is played; there are also regular themed disco evenings.
🔳 Off map ✉ Via Mercati 24b ☎ 055 477 978 🚌 4

ESTATE FIESOLANA

estatefiesolana.it

This season of music, opera and ballet is primarily held in Fiesole's open-air Teatro Romano (▷ 97), from late June to September. Head for the hills for an unbeatable experience.
Estate Fiesolana ☎ Contact APT (tourist information), Fiesole 055 596 1323
Teatro Romano ✉ Via Marini 🚌 7

GIRASOL

girasol.it

Florentines love Latin-American bars. This is the best, with live and recorded Cuban, Caribbean and other music from the region.
🔳 D1 ✉ Via del Romito 1r ☎ 055 474 948 🚌 14

NELSON MANDELA FORUM

mandelaforum.it

This medium-size venue near Campo di Marte hosts some of Italy's most celebrated rock and pop acts. Check in advance for British and US bands who may be playing here.
🔳 M4 ✉ Viale Pasquale Paoli 3 🎫 Box office Via Alamanini 055 678 841 for tickets 🚌 3, 10

PISCINA LE PAVONIERE

lepavoniere.it

Located within the peaceful Cascine park (▷ 98), the Peacock is the most popular—and the prettiest—outdoor swimming pool in Florence. The park's trees provide welcome shade on hot days.
🔳 A4 ✉ Viale della Catena 3 ☎ 055 362 233 🕐 Summer only, daily 10–7 🚌 17, tram

TENAX

tenax.org

Warehouse-style Tenax is a Florentine clubbers' institution near Vespucci airport, offering a continually evolving mix of live bands and house sounds from the resident DJ and internationally known mixers. The Nobody's Perfect Party on Saturdays is *the* night out in the city.
🔳 Off map ✉ Via Pratese 46 ☎ 055 308 160 🕐 Fri–Sat until 4am. Closed mid-May to Sep 🚌 29, 30

FOOTBALL IS ALL

Many Florentines take more pride in their football (soccer) team than in their artistic heritage. Until 2002 AC Fiorentina, also known as the "Viola" (the Purples), were one of the top clubs in Italy, but following a financial scandal the club was declared bankrupt and demoted three divisions. The team clawed its way back into Serie A and regained its former glory. Games take place at the Stadio Artemio Franchi, where you can join the ever-faithful fans cheering on the lads in lavender.

Where to Eat

NATURALLY ROBUST

The classic Florentine dish is *bistecca alla fiorentina* (T-bone steak sold by the weight, usually 100g). Grilled and served rare with lemon wedges, it can be found on the menu in many Florentine restaurants. Other traditional dishes include *trippa alla fiorentina* (tripe stewed with tomatoes and served with Parmesan), *crostini* (toasted bread with a variety of toppings) and *panzanella* (a salad of crumbled bread tossed with tomatoes with olive oil, onions, basil and parsley).

LE CAVE DI MAIANO (€€–€€€)

Located just below Fiesole, the lovely patio terrace of this restaurant looks down over Florence, a perfect place for a summer dinner. Tuck into pasta with porcini mushrooms or wild boar sauce and perfectly grilled *bistecca* (steak) accompanied by a good Chianti.

⊞ Off map ✉ Via delle Cave di Maiano 16 ☎ 055 591 33 🕐 Daily 12.30–3, 7.30–10.30 🚌 7

IL FIESOLANO (PERSEUS) (€€)

casatrattoria.com

This is one of Fiesole's best restaurants in which to sample the famous *bistecca alla fiorentina* (T-bone steak, ▷ panel). Other classic Tuscan dishes are served on a terrace at the back, facing the Teatro Romano in Fiesole.

⊞ Off map ✉ Piazza Mino da Fiesole 9 ☎ 055 59143 🕐 Mon–Sat 12.30–2.30, 7.30–10.30 🚌 7

FUORI PORTA (€–€€)

fuoriporta.it

If you're walking up the hill to Piazzale Michelangelo (▷ 88) make sure you take a break at this lovely wine bar with its terrace overlooking the old city gate of San Miniato. Food specials include pasta, salads, *carpacci* (fine slices of tender raw steak) or the classic house *crostoni*, a grilled cheese sandwich. The wine list features more than 500 labels, with over 50 available by the glass. Fine

Tuscan reds dominate, alongside a huge range of *grappe*.

⊞ G8 ✉ Via Monte alle Croci 10 ☎ 055 234 2483 🕐 Daily noon–11.30 🚌 D

LA LOGGIA, VILLA SAN MICHELE (€€€)

belmond.com

The evocative former monastery setting and some of the finest cuisine in the area attract diners to this elegant restaurant in the Villa San Michele. The views take in the whole city.

⊞ Off map ✉ Via Doccia 4 ☎ 055 567 8200 🕐 Daily 1–2.30, 7.30–10.30; closed end Nov to end Mar 🚌 7

POVERO PESCE (€€–€€€)

Considering the price of fish in Italy, this unpretentious fish and seafood restaurant, east of Santa Croce, is a real find. A meal might typically consist of an *antipasto misto* of five or six little fishy tasters, then perhaps spaghetti *alle vongole* (with clams) followed by a grilled fish—the menu depends on what is available at the market that day. It tends to get very full in the evenings.

⊞ L5 ✉ Via Pier Fortunato Calvi 8r ☎ 055 671218 🕐 Daily noon–3, 7–11 🚌 10, 82

Florence is one of Italy's top destinations and hotels are, on the whole, expensive. Check online to see what deals are available, and, if possible, visit out of season.

Introduction

Choose from world-class hotels in historic buildings, ultrachic boutique hotels, family-run *pensiones* that haven't changed in decades—or rent a room in a private house.

Hotels
Tuscan hotels (*alberghi*) are graded by the regional authorities on a star rating of one to five. These refer to the facilities provided rather than character or comfort. Expect five- and four-star hotels to be grand, with superb facilities and service. Three-star hotels are more idiosyncratic. Prices can vary enormously, as can the public areas and staffing levels; but all rooms will have a TV, phone and private bathroom. One and two stars are relatively inexpensive, clean and comfortable, and rooms almost always have private bathrooms in two-star places. Air conditioning is normally provided from two stars and up. Breakfast is usually included but can be very basic.

Rooms to Rent
Signs saying rooms (*camere* or *zimmer*) are rooms to rent in private houses and are a good option if money is tight or you can't find a hotel. Local tourist offices keep a list.

Where to Stay
Florence is so compact that if you stay in the historic centre all the main sights will be on your doorstep. Staying farther out will usually be less expensive and you may still be able to walk into town—from Piazzale Michelangelo, for example, it's only 20 minutes to the Duomo.

RESERVATIONS

Florence is so popular that you will need to book in advance at whatever time of year you decide to visit. If you're booking in advance from home, make certain you get written confirmation and take it with you. Without this, you may turn up and find all knowledge of your booking denied. If you make an internet booking, print out your booking confirmation and take it with you.

From top: the Westin Excelsior; the Scoti; bags waiting to be picked up; Loggiato dei Serviti

Budget Hotels

PRICES

Expect to pay up to €130 per night in high season for a double room in a budget hotel.

CAMPING

Campeggio Michelangelo, on the hills south of the Arno, is just a short bus ride from central Florence. It has hot showers, toilets, washing machines, electricity points, internet access, a supermarket and a bar that looks out over the city. There are 240 pitches and it's open all year.

➕ H8 ✉ Viale Michelangelo 80 ☎ 055 681 1977 🚌 12, 13

CASA PUCCI

casapucci.it

Steps from the lovely Piazza Santo Spirito and its lively nightlife, Signora Pucci's home occupies an ex-convent and offers five home-like bedrooms, one with a four-poster. There's a kitchen that guests can use and a large court-yard garden for summer breakfasts.

➕ D6 ✉ Via Santa Monaca 8 ☎ 055 216 560 🚌 C3, D

CASA SCHLATTER

casaschlatter-florence.com

Although this ex-artists' residence is a little way from the city centre, bus links are good. The three guest rooms are individually furnished with antiques, and there is a pretty garden. The breakfast is delicious.

➕ J3 ✉ Viale dei Mille 14 ☎ 347 118 0215 🚌 10, 17

CESTELLI

hotelcestelli.com

Owned by a Florentine-Japanese couple, the Cestelli is a friendly gem close to the chic shops of Via de' Tornabuoni. The rooms are simply furnished but pristine, with old parquet floors and some antiques. Not all have bathrooms and no breakfast is provided.

➕ E6 ✉ Borgo SS Apostoli 25 ☎ 055 214 213 🚌 C3, D

JOHANNA I

antichedimorefiorentine.it

Occupying the first floor of a gracious 19th-century building near San Lorenzo and beautifully renovated, the 10 rooms are small but nicely furnished and there is a communal room with a fridge.

➕ G3 ✉ Via Bonifacio Lupi 14 ☎ 055 481 896 🚌 C2

SCOTI

hotelscoti.com

The Scoti is housed in an atmospheric 15th-century building in an excellent location directly opposite the Palazzo Strozzi, in the shopping haven of Via de' Tornabuoni. In addition, it offers great value and tons of period character. The 11 bedrooms are simple and light, and the lounge area has attractive 18th-century frescoes depicting Italian landscapes.

➕ E6 ✉ Via de' Tornabuoni 7 ☎ 055 292 128 🚌 C3

VILLA BETANIA

villabetania.it

Immersed in a beautiful garden, this ochre-coloured villa offers excellent value, fresh air and breakfast on the ter-race in summer. Each of the 20 rooms is furnished in its own individual style but all are very clean, and the staff are friendly. A 10-minute walk downhill (or a bus ride) brings you to Porta Romana.

➕ D9 ✉ Viale del Poggio Imperiale 23 ☎ 055 222 243 🚌 38

Mid-Range Hotels

AD ASTRA

adastraflorence.it

This beautiful hotel, housed on the upper floors of a lovely villa, overlooks the Giardini Torrigiani, Florence's largest privately owned garden. The decor combines classic elegance with some quirky retro touches; the rooms are supremely comfortable and the breakfast delicious.
➕ D7 ✉ Via del Campuccio 53 ☎ 055 057 0602 🚌 D

ANNALENA

annalenahotel.com

In a Medici palazzo opposite the Boboli Gardens, this hotel was once the haunt of artists and writers. Some of the 20 rooms have terraces and views of the private Annalena gardens. It's a lovely, peaceful spot.
➕ D8 ✉ Via Romana 34 ☎ 055 222 402 🚌 36, 37, D

ANTICA DIMORE JOHLEA

antichedimorefiorentine.it

One of the assets of this six-room B&B is its panoramic roof terrace. The rooms

are all beautifully done out with antiques and vibrant fabrics, and most have four-poster beds. There's a sitting room with an honesty bar.
➕ G3 ✉ Via San Gallo 80 ☎ 055 463 3292 🚌 C1, 1, 6, 11

CASA HOWARD

casahoward.com

Attention to detail, superb service and a lot of little extras are the hallmarks of this wonderful guest house, handily situated near Santa Maria Novella. Breakfast is served in your room.
➕ D4 ✉ Via della Scala 18 ☎ 06 6992 4555 🚌 C3

CASCI

hotelcasci.com

Now a family-run hotel, with 24 immaculate rooms, this old palazzo close to the Duomo was once home to the Italian composer Gioacchino Rossini. Although modernized, it still has some of its original 14th-century features.
➕ F4 ✉ Via Cavour 13 ☎ 055 211 686 🚌 C1

DAVANZATI

hoteldavanzati.it

You can't beat the location of this small hotel near Piazza della Signoria. Rooms are simply furnished but spotless; bathrooms are modern. Complimentary extras include iPads, hot drinks and cakes at teatime, and Happy Hour.
➕ F6 ✉ Via Porta Rossa 5 ☎ 055 286 666 🚌 C3, D

LOGGIATO DEI SERVITI

loggiatodeiservitihotel.it

You can relax under vaulted ceilings, amid dark-wood antiques and rich fabrics in the former monastery of the Serviti. The 37 rooms are enlivened by bright curtains and throws. Many look onto the arcades of Piazza Santissima Annunziata and the breakfast room has views of the Accademia gardens.

🏠 G4 ✉ Piazza Santissima Annunziata 3 ☎ 055 289 592 🚌 C1, C2, 6

MARIO'S

hotelmarios.com

This family-run hotel exemplifies the great value for money that can still be found in this expensive city. It feels as if you are staying in someone's home, with care and attention paid to the 16 atmospheric rooms and to your needs.

🏠 E4 ✉ Via Faenza 89 ☎ 055 216 801 🚌 T1

MILU

hotelmilu.com

You can step outside onto Florence's most elegant street from this boutique hotel. The tranquil rooms have clean lines with notes of vibrant colour. The hotel doubles as an art gallery, with many works on sale.

🏠 E5 ✉ Via de' Tornabuoni 8 ☎ 055 217 103 🚌 C2

PALAZZO GALLETTI

palazzogalletti.it

This 11-room hotel occupies the first floor of a 16th-century palazzo. The smart bedrooms are a mix of old and new; most have small balconies overlooking the internal courtyard. The two suites are huge and feature original floor-to-ceiling frescoes.

🏠 G5 ✉ Via Sant'Egidio 12 ☎ 055 390 5750 🚌 C1, C2

LA SCALETTA

hotellascaletta.com

For those who want to stay on the quieter south side of the River Arno,

La Scaletta is a good choice. The hotel is just steps away from the Ponte Vecchio, the Pitti Palace and the Boboli Gardens. The rooms have a home-like feel and there is a lovely rooftop terrace.

🏠 E7 ✉ Via de Guicciardini 13 ☎ 055 283 028 🚌 D

SOPRARNO SUITES

soprarnosuites.com

Inhabiting two floors of a Renaissance palazzo in the Oltrarno, this gorgeous hotel has 11 highly individual rooms featuring lofty, frescoed ceilings, an intriguing collection of retro furnishings, in-room bathtubs and fabulous bathrooms. Breakfast—with homemade cakes—is delicious.

🏠 E7 ✉ Via Maggio 35 ☎ 055 046 8719 🚌 C3, D

TORNABUONI BEACCI

tornabuonihotels.com

Well-placed for shopping and sightseeing, this handsome hotel has a large, leafy roof garden and antiques-filled lounge, which are quiet retreats from the bustle of the city outside on this busy street. The 60 bedrooms are simple and uncluttered, decorated with antique furnishings.

🏠 E6 ✉ Via de' Tornabuoni 3 ☎ 055 212 645 🚌 C2, C3

VILLA FIESOLE

villafiesole.it

In the hilltop village of Fiesole, this hotel with 32 rooms has an outdoor pool and a wonderful Victorian greenhouse that accommodates the breakfast room, a lounge area and several bedrooms. This hotel offers really good value for great surroundings.

🏠 Off map at M1 ✉ Via Beato Angelico 35 ☎ 055 597 252 🚌 7

Luxury Hotels

PRICES
Expect to pay over €300 per night in high season for a double room in a luxury hotel.

FOUR SEASONS FLORENCE
fourseasons.com/florence
It may be a little way from the centre, but the service and facilities at this luxury resort more than compensate. Apart from the magnificent public rooms and bedrooms, there is a huge garden, a fabulous spa and gym and a Michelin-starred restaurant.

✚ H4 ✉ Borgo Pinti 99 ☎ Toll free 800 791 490; from the US 1 800 819 5053 🚌 6, 8, 14

HELVETIA & BRISTOL
hotelhelvetiabristol.com
With its old-world atmosphere and great location near the Duomo, this grand 18th-century hotel is an excellent choice. All the rooms are decorated with opulent fabrics and antique furnishings. The belle époque winter garden is the main dining room—come here for breakfast or lunch, or for chef Pasquale D'Ambrosio's cooking in the evening.

✚ E5 ✉ Via dei Pescioni 2 ☎ 055 266 51 🚌 C2

J. K. PLACE
jkplace.com
This small, chic hotel is a fabulous blend of old and new, where modern art is cleverly displayed alongside antique features. The sleek bedrooms and comfortable day rooms are decorated with great attention to detail. There's a pleasant rooftop terrace on Piazza Santa Maria Novella.

✚ E5 ✉ Piazza Santa Maria Novella 7 ☎ 055 264 5181 🚌 All buses to Santa Maria Novella station

PORTRAIT FIRENZE
lungarnocollection.com
For the ultimate in luxury and a magnificent riverside location, book into Ferragamo-owned Portrait Firenze. The soft grey rooms all have mini kitchens and the latest in high-tech gadgetry.

✚ F6 ✉ Lungarno degli Acciaiuoli 4 ☎ 055 2726 8000 🚌 C3, D

ST. REGIS FLORENCE
stregisflorence.com
Florence's opulent St. Regis occupies a 19th-century palazzo on the north bank of the Arno with 107 gorgeously decorated rooms, the best of which have a river view. The myriad facilities include a spa and a Michelin-starred restaurant, the Winter Garden.

✚ D5 ✉ Piazza Ognissanti 1 ☎ 055 271 61 🚌 A, B

SAVOY
roccofortehotels.com
The Savoy enjoys a fabulous location right on Piazza della Repubblica and steps from the Duomo. It offers stylish, understated luxury in its 80 rooms and suites, plus a cocktail bar and restaurant with a terrace right on the buzzing square.

✚ F5 ✉ Piazza della Repubblica 7 ☎ 055 27351 🚌 C2

WESTIN EXCELSIOR
westinflorence.com
A hotel in the grand style, the 171-room Westin Excelsior is located right on the Arno; try to book one of the many rooms with watery views. Top-floor gourmet restaurant SE.STO (▷ 50) has views of the whole city; book in for a sunset cocktail at the very least.

✚ D5 ✉ Piazza Ognissanti 3 ☎ 055 271 51 🚌 C3, D

This section covers all the practical aspects of your trip, including how to get there, how to get around and useful information for when you're there.

Planning Ahead

When to Go

Florence's peak season runs from March to October, although many consider it virtually uninterrupted. The city is overrun with tour groups in May, June and July. If you like heat, go in August—although many Florentines are on holiday and some restaurants close, it's a good time to go because everything is quieter.

AVERAGE DAILY MAXIMUM TEMPERATURES

JAN	FEB	MAR	APR	MAY	JUN	JUL	AUG	SEP	OCT	NOV	DEC
50°F	52°F	59°F	64°F	73°F	79°F	84°F	82°F	79°F	70°F	57°F	54°F
10°C	11°C	15°C	18°C	23°C	26°C	29°C	28°C	26°C	21°C	14°C	12°C

Spring (March to May) is a good time to visit if you want to avoid the summer heat.
Summer (June to August) can be extremely hot and humid, often uncomfortably so in July and August.
Autumn (September to November) is generally the wettest time in Tuscany, and thunderstorms are common in September.
Winter (December to February) temperatures are often chilly, and rainfall can be high. However, the city is at its emptiest at this time (if you avoid Christmas and New Year).

WHAT'S ON

January *Pitti Immagine:* Fashion shows at the Fortezza da Basso.
February *Carnevale:* A low-key version of Venice's annual extravaganza.
March *Festa dell'Annunziata* (25 Mar): Traditionally the Florentine new year, with a fair to celebrate in Piazza Santissima Annunziata.
Scoppio del Carro: The Easter Sunday service at the Duomo culminates in an exploding carriage full of fireworks.
April *Mostra Mercato Internazionale dell' Artigianato:* An international arts and crafts festival in the Fortezza da Basso.
May/June *Maggio Musicale:* Florence's international music and dance festival.
Festa del Grillo (Sun after Ascension): Crickets are sold in cages, then released in the park of Le Cascine (▷ 98).
June *Calcio in Costume:* An elaborate soccer game between town districts, played in medieval costume in Piazza Santa Croce; preceded by a procession.
Festa di San Giovanni (24 Jun): Fireworks in Piazzale Michelangelo (▷ 87) celebrate the feast of Florence's patron saint.
Estate Fiesolana (mid-Jun to Sep): A Fiesole arts festival.
September *Festa del Rificolona* (7 Sep): Children carry paper lanterns in Piazza Santissima Annunziata to honour the birth of the Virgin.
October *Amici della Musica* (Oct–Apr): Concerts. Tickets from Teatro della Pergola (☎ 055 226 4316).
November *Festival dei Popoli* (Nov–Dec): A film festival in the Odeon Cinehall (▷ 46), showing international films.

Florence Online

enit.it
Florence is particularly well covered on the Italian Tourist Board website, with information on history, culture, events, accommodation and gastronomy, in several languages.

visittuscany.com
Run by the Tuscan Regional Tourist Board, this site covers the whole region, including Florence.

comune.fi.it
Florence City Council site has good information in English. Its tourism, museum and art pages are always up to date, with some good links.

firenzeturismo.it
The official APT tourism site with plenty of useful information in English.

firenze.net
This Florence-based site, in Italian and English, has information on where to go and what to do, with good maps and plenty of links.

emmeti.it
Another Italy-based site, in Italian and English, with a good range of information and links for Florence. It is strong on local events and has an online hotel reservation service.

initaly.com
This lively US site is clearly run by passionate Italophiles and has excellent planning tips and sightseeing hints.

florence.hotelsfinder.com
Useful online hotel booking site for Florence and other Italian destinations.

firenzemusei.it
You can reserve a timed entrance ticket, to avoid a long wait, to the main Florentine museums, including the Uffizi, via this efficient website.

INTERNET ACCESS

Florence is rapidly coming into the 21st-century with its online facilities. WiFi hotspots can be found all over the city, including Piazza Duomo, Piazza della Repubblica, Piazza della Signoria, Piazza Santo Spirito and Santa Maria Novella station. Many bars, cafés and restaurants offer free internet access, as do most hotels.

Getting There

DIRECT FLIGHTS

There are no direct intercontinental flights to Florence so visitors have to fly to Milan (298km/185 miles north), Rome (277km/172 miles south) or another European city, then take a connecting flight or train. The flight from New York to Rome takes around nine hours; there are two daily direct trains to Florence from the airport, leaving at 11.08 and 3.08 with a journey time of 2 hours 15 minutes.

AIRPORTS

You can choose from three airports—Galileo Galilei Airport at Pisa, the small Amerigo Vespucci Airport at Florence and Guglielmo Marconi Airport at Bologna. The flight takes approximately 2 hours from London.

120km (75 miles)

Florence Airport
4km (2.5 miles) to central
Florence
Bus, 20 minutes

Bologna Airport
105km (65 miles) to
Florence
Bus then train, 1 hour

Pisa Airport
80km (50 miles) to
Florence
Train, 1 hour 15 minutes

ENTRY REQUIREMENTS

Check the latest passport and visa information before you travel; look up the British embassy website at gov.uk/government/world/italy or the United States embassy at usembassy.gov. EU citizens do not require visas to visit Italy.

CUSTOMS REGULATIONS

● EU nationals do not have to declare goods imported for their personal use.
● The limits for non-EU visitors are 200 cigarettes or 100 small cigars or 250g of tobacco; 1 litre of alcohol (over 22 per cent alcohol) or 2 litres of fortified wine; 60ml of perfume.

FROM FLORENCE AIRPORT

Amerigo Vespucci Airport (tel 055 306 1830, aeroporto.firenze.it), also known as Peretola, is 4km (2.5 miles) northwest of the city. It handles domestic and European flights. The airport is connected to the city centre by the light blue Volainbus shuttle (administered by BusItalia Nord, tel 800 424 500, fsbusitalia.it), which runs every 30 minutes from 6am to 8.30pm, then every hour until 11.30pm, to Santa Maria Novella station. The journey takes 20 minutes and tickets, which cost €6, can be bought on board. Taxis cost around €22, plus possible surcharges (agree a price before you set off).

FROM PISA AIRPORT

Pisa's Galileo Galilei Airport (tel 050 849 300, pisa-airport.com), the region's main point of entry, lies 80km (50 miles) west of Florence. The one spacious terminal handles domestic and European flights. The airport is 1km (0.5 miles) from Pisa Centrale station, which links with all Italian network rail destinations. The station is connected to the airport by a People Mover, a driverless train that leaves from just outside the airport. Its trains run every 6–8 minutes from 6am to 6pm; tickets cost €3.50 and are available in the arrivals hall. A single onward train ticket to Florence costs €8.70. Caronna Tour run Sky Line buses from Pisa to Florence every 90 minutes from 8am to 11.30pm; journey time is 1 hour, tickets cost €7 and can be purchased in the arrivals hall. A taxi to Florence could cost you more than €130. There is a helpful information office inside the terminal where you can buy tickets for trains and the bus.

FROM BOLOGNA AIRPORT

Guglielmo Marconi Airport (tel 051 647 9615, bologna-airport.it) is 105km (65 miles) north-east of Florence in the Emilia-Romagna region and handles a large volume of European charter and scheduled flights, as well as budget airline flights. A shuttle bus costing about €6 takes passengers to Bologna Centrale station (trenitalia.com). From here the journey takes about 35 minutes and costs around €20, depending on the type of train taken. Make sure your ticket is valid for the right train. Rental cars are available in Terminal A. Taxis to Florence cost about €220.

ARRIVING BY TRAIN

The main station, Santa Maria Novella (trenitalia.com), has links with major Italian cities. Most buses in Florence depart from the station forecourt, and there are usually taxis waiting. Don't forget to validate your ticket, by inserting it into the yellow box on the platform, before boarding your train. Fast services that don't terminate in Florence may stop at Campo di Marte station instead, which is just outside the ring road, near the football stadium; catch another train to Santa Maria Novella from here.

ARRIVING BY LONG-DISTANCE BUS

Lazzi runs express services to and from Rome and links Florence with major European cities as part of the Eurolines network (tel 0 892 899 091, eurolines.eu).

TRAVEL INSURANCE

Take out your insurance as soon as you book your trip to ensure you are covered for delays. Most policies cover cancellation, medical expenses, accident compensation, personal liability and loss of personal belongings (including money). Your policy should cover the cost of getting you home in case of medical emergency. An annual travel policy may be the best value if you intend to make several trips in a year away from home, but long trips abroad may not be covered. If you have private medical coverage, check your policy, as you may be covered while you are away.

CAR RENTAL

The major car rental groups are all represented in the region and have offices at airports, rail stations and in the bigger cities.

Getting Around

VISITORS WITH DISABILITIES

As in many other historic Italian cities, visitors with disabilities are far from well served in Florence, though things are improving. The official APT website (▷ 115) has detailed information for tourists with special needs. Many city museums are fully wheelchair-accessible, with ramps, elevators and suitable bathrooms. The grey and green buses can take wheelchairs, as does the electric D bus, which goes through the heart of Florence (board via the electric platform at the rear door). Taxis do take wheelchairs but it is wise to let them know when you make a reservation.

The Tuscan capital has no metro or subway system, but the *centro storico* (historic centre) is largely traffic-free and can be crossed on foot in 30 minutes. There is an efficient bus service linking the outskirts of the city to the central areas, and a fleet of small electric buses serves the *centro storico*. The city is in the middle of major work to install a tram system. The first phase, linking Santa Maria Novella station with the western suburb of Scandicci, is complete; two more routes are under construction. Azienda Trasporti Area Fiorentina (ATAF) is responsible for public transportation (ataf.net).

BUSES

Bus routes in Florence are numbered and many start and end at the railway station at regular intervals. The zippy little electric buses that run through the *centro storico*, identified by letters (C1, C2, C3 and D), link all kinds of places in the narrow streets of the old city. Buy tickets at bars, tobacconists and from the ATAF booth on Piazza Stazione before boarding. Once on board, insert your ticket into the small orange box and it will be stamped with the time. Failure to validate your ticket can result in a hefty fine. The ticket is valid for the next 90 minutes for any bus; it costs €1.50 or €2.50 if purchased on board. A multiple ticket gives you ten 90-minute tickets and costs €14. The tourist information office by the station has bus maps.

HOP-ON-HOP-OFF BUS

If you really want to avoid any leg work, or want an overview of how the city is laid out, take an open-top bus ride with City Sightseeing (tel 055 290 451, city-sightseeing.it). This bus permits visitors to get on and off at any number of designated stops on the tourist itinerary. The ticket is valid for 24 hours and costs €23.

LONG-DISTANCE BUS

Buses covering the rest of Tuscany from Florence are operated by the umbrella company CAP, which incorporates several bus companies:

• SITA serves southern and eastern Tuscany
• CAP serves the region to the northeast of Florence

For full information, follow the links on the Trasporti Toscana page at lazzi.it.

TAXIS

The official white Florentine taxis are clean and comfortable. You cannot hail them on the street; instead you must pick them up at a taxi rank at key locations such as the station, Piazza del Duomo, Piazza della Repubblica, or call one of the official cab companies: Radio Taxi 4242 (tel 055 4242 SMS or WhatsApp 39 334 662 2550) or Radio Taxi 4390 (tel 055 4390). The meter starts running the moment your call is received. Supplements are charged for baggage and at night.

BICYCLES AND MOTORCYCLES

Bicycles can be rented from Florence by Bike at Via San Zanobi 54r (tel 055 488 992, florencebybike.it).

Mopeds and motorcycles can be rented from Alinari at Via Zanobi 38r (tel 055 280 500, alinarirental.com).

CARS

It is really not worth driving around Florence. Much of the city is closed to traffic, there is a one-way system and parking is difficult. However, a car is ideal if you plan to tour the Tuscan countryside. If you do rent a car, try to book a hotel with parking.

Main car rental companies are:
• Avis, Borgo Ognissanti 128r, tel 055 213 629.
• Europcar, Borgo Ognissanti 53–55r, tel 055 290 438.
• Hertz Italiana, Borgo Ognissanti 137, tel 055 239 8205.

Driving around outside the city is easy. Tolls are payable on highways (*autostrade*). Most, but by no means all, fuel stations take credit cards. You can contact Highway emergency/Breakdown service (ACI) on 803 116.

Essential Facts

- The Florentines' preferred newspaper is *La Nazione*, a national paper produced in Florence.
- You can buy foreign newspapers and magazines at the station and at Sorbi, the kiosk in Piazza della Signoria.

The euro is the official currency of Italy. Bank notes come in denominations of €5, €10, €20, €50, €100 and €200, and coins in denominations of 1, 2, 5, 10, 20 and 50 cents and €1 and €2.

UK visitors should check the very latest entry requirements as a result of the country's decision to leave the EU. Check if a visa is required along with a valid passport and if reduced-cost medical treatment with the European Health Insurance Card (EHIC) is still available. Visit gov.uk/visit-europe-brexit.

ELECTRICITY
- Voltage is 220 volts and sockets take two round pins.

EMERGENCY TELEPHONE NUMBERS
- Police: 113; 112 (Carabinieri)
- Fire: 115
- Ambulance: 118
- State Police headquarters is on Via Zara 2 (tel 055 497 71).

ETIQUETTE
- Make the effort to speak some Italian; it will be appreciated.
- Shake hands on introduction and leaving; once you know people better you can replace this with a kiss on each cheek.
- Use the polite form for "you", *lei*, unless the other person uses *tu*.
- Always say *buon giorno* (hello) and *arrivederci* (goodbye) in shops.
- Italians do not get drunk in public.
- Smoking is banned in enclosed public spaces.

LOST PROPERTY
- Lost property office: Via Veracini 5 (tel 055 334 802, open Mon, Wed, Fri 8.30–12.30; Tue, Thu 8.30–12.30, 2.30–4).
- Report losses of passports to the police and other items to the Questura at Via Zara 2 (tel 055 49771).
- There's also a lost property office at Stazione Santa Maria Novella (tel 055 235 6120, open daily 4.15pm–1.30am).

MAIL
- Main post office: Via Pellicceria 3 (tel 055 273 6481, poste.it, open Mon–Sat 8.15–7).
- There is another big post office at Via Pietrapiana 53–55 (tel 055 267 4231, open Mon–Fri 8.15–7, Sat 8.15–12.30).
- Stamps (*francobolli*) can be purchased from post offices or from tobacconists displaying a white T sign on a black or blue background.
- Post boxes are small, red and marked "Poste"

or "Lettere." The slot on the left is for addresses within the city and the slot on the right is for other destinations.

MEDICINES AND MEDICAL TREATMENT
● EU nationals receive reduced-cost medical treatment on production of the relevant document (EHIC card for Britons, at least until Brexit is finalized). Private medical insurance for UK and all other nationals is still advised.
● For medical emergencies, call 118.
● Medical Service Firenze (Via Roma 4, tel 055 475 411, medicalservice.firenze.it) has English-speaking doctors. Phone for an appointment or call out, or just drop in to the walk-in clinic (Mon–Fri 11–12, 1–3, 5–6, Sat 11–12, 1–3).
● Hospital: Santa Maria Nuova is at Piazza Santa Maria Nuova 1, call 055 69381.
● Interpreters can be arranged for free through Ospedale di Careggi (surgical accident and emergency unit) at Viale Pieraccini 17 (tel 055 794 111/ 7057, Mon–Sat 8.30–12.30). They can also advise if you need dental services.
● Pharmacies are indicated by a large green or red cross. For pharmacy information, call 800 420 707 (toll-free from within Italy).
● All-night pharmacies:
Comunale 13 della Stazione, at the train station (tel 055 216 761); All'Insegna del Moro-Taverna, Piazza San Giovanni 20r (tel 055 211 343); Molteni, at Via dei Calzaiuoli 7r (tel 055 284 530).

MONEY AND CREDIT CARDS
● Credit cards are widely accepted.
● ATMs are plentiful.

NATIONAL HOLIDAYS
● 1 Jan: New Year's Day; 6 Jan: Epiphany; Easter Sunday; Easter Monday; 25 Apr: Liberation Day; 1 May: Labour Day; 2 Jun: Repubblica Day; 24 June: Feast of San Giovanni (Florence only);15 Aug: Assumption; 1 Nov: All Saints' Day; 8 Dec: Immaculate Conception; 25 Dec: Christmas Day; 26 Dec: St. Stephen's Day.

TOILETS
● Italian toilets are generally improving both in cleanliness and facilities.
● Expect to pay about €1 to use the toilet. Those away from the main tourist areas are usually free.
● There are 22 public toilets in Piazza San Giovanni, near the Baptistery.
● Most bars and cafés have toilets and usually allow anybody to use them (although it's polite to have at least a drink).
● Florence has promoted the initiative "Courtesy Point" in which several bars and cafés have made their toilets available to the public.

CONSULATES
British Embassy Consular Section ✉ Via XX Settembre 80/a, Rome ☎ 06 4220 0001
Portuguese Consul ✉ Via Colonetta 5, Milan ☎ 02 545 5553
Spanish Honorary Consul ✉ Vía dei Servi 13 ☎ 055 212 207
US Consulate ✉ Lungarno Amerigo Vespucci 38 ☎ 055 266 951

PRECAUTIONS

● Take care of wallets, handbags and backpacks as pickpockets target tourists.
● Keep a copy of the front page of your passport.
● List the numbers and expiration dates of your credit cards and keep the list separately.
● If a theft occurs, make a statement (*denuncia*) at a police station within 24 hours if you wish to make an insurance claim.
● After dark avoid Le Cascine and the station.

OPENING TIMES

● Banks: generally Mon–Fri 8.30–1.30, 2.30–4. Some banks also open Saturday mornings.
● Post offices: Mon–Fri 8.15–1.30, Sat 8.15–12.30.
● Shops: normally Mon–Sat 8.30–1 and from 3 or 4 until 7 or 8; larger stores in city centre 10–7.
● Museums: see individual entries.
● Churches: 7 or 8–12.30 and then from 3 or 4 until 7.30. Main tourist attractions often stay open longer. No two are the same.

TELEPHONES

● Public phones are silver and orange, but these are few and far between.
● Few public telephones take coins. Phone cards (*carta* or *scheda* or *tessera telefonica*) are the most practical way to use a public phone.
● Directory inquiries: call 1254.
● International directory inquiries: call 1254.
● International operator: call 1254; you can also make reverse charge international calls on this number via the operator.
● Cheap rate is all day Sunday and 9pm–8am (national) on other days; 10pm–8am (international).
● To call Italy from the UK, dial 00 followed by 39 (the code for Italy) then the number. To call the UK from Italy dial 00 44 then drop the first zero from the area code.
● To call Italy from the US dial 011 followed by 39. To call the US from Italy dial 00 1.
● Florence's area code (055) must always be dialled even if you are calling from within Florence.

TOURIST INFORMATION OFFICES

● The principal tourist office can be found at Via Cavour 1r (tel 055 290 832/3, firenzeturismo. it, Mon–Fri 9–1).
● Another useful information point is at Piazza Stazione 4 (tel 055 212 245, Mon–Sat 9–7, Sun 9–2; email turismo3@comune.fi.it).

Language

Italian pronunciation is totally consistent. Cs and gs are hard when they are followed by an a, o or u (as in "cat" and "got"), and soft if followed by an e or an i (as in "child" or "geranium"). The Tuscans often pronounce their cs and chs as hs.

USEFUL WORDS AND PHRASES

buon giorno	good morning
buona sera	good afternoon/ evening
buona notte	good night
ciao	hello/ goodbye (informal)
arrivederci	goodbye (informal)
arrivederla	goodbye (formal)
per favore	please
grazie	thank you
prego	you're welcome
come sta/stai?	how are you?
sto bene	I'm fine
mi dispiace	I'm sorry
scusi/scusa	excuse me/ I beg your pardon
permesso	excuse me (in a crowd)
quant'è?	how much is it?
quando?	when?
avete...?	do you have...?
qui/qua	here

BASIC VOCABULARY

sì	yes
no	no
non ho capito	I don't understand
sinistra	left
destra	right
entrata	entrance
uscita	exit
aperto	open
chiuso	closed
buono	good
cattivo	bad
grande	big
piccolo	small
con	with
senza	without
più	more

NUMBERS

uno/primo	1/first
due/ secondo	2/second
tre/terzo	3/third
quattro/ quarto	4/fourth
cinque/ quinto	5/fifth
sei	6
sette	7
otto	8
nove	9
dieci	10
venti	20
cinquanta	50
cento	100
mille	1,000
milione	1,000,000

EMERGENCIES

aiuto!	help!
dov'è il telefono più vicino?	where is the nearest telephone?
c'è stato un incidente	there has been an accident
chiamate la polizia	call the police
chiamate un medico/ un'ambulanza	call a doctor/ an ambulance
pronto soccorso	first aid
dov'è l'ospedale più vicino?	where is the nearest hospital?

Timeline

THE FLORIN

Florence minted its own coins, florins, in silver in 1235 and in gold in 1252. Soon they were being used as the standard coin in Europe, evidence of the pre-eminence of Florence in European finance.

BEFORE 1000

Florence started to grow in 59BC as a result of an agrarian law passed by Julius Caesar, granting land to retired army veterans. Byzantine walls were added to the Roman walls in AD541–44, as protection against the Ostrogoths. The Lombards took Tuscany in 570 but were defeated in the early ninth century by Charlemagne. Florence then became part of the Holy Roman Empire, ruled by imperial princes known as Margraves.

1115 The first comune (city state) is formed. Florence is run by a 100-strong assembly.

1250–60 The Primo Popolo regime controls Florence, dominated by trade guilds.

1296 The building of the Duomo begins, under Arnolfo di Cambio.

1340s Florence faces economic crisis after Edward III of England bankrupts the Peruzzi and Bardi and the Black Death plague halves the population.

1406 Florence captures Pisa, gaining direct access to the sea.

1458 Cosimo de' Medici is recognized as ruler of Florence.

1469–92 Lorenzo the Magnificent rules.

1494 Florence surrenders to Charles VIII of France. Savonarola, a zealous monk, takes control of the city.

1498 Savonarola is burned at the stake after four years of rule, and Florence becomes a republic.

1502 The Republic of Florence retakes Pisa.

1570 Cosimo I creates a Tuscan state free from the Holy Roman Empire.

1743 Anna Maria Luisa, last of the Medici, dies. Florence is then ruled by the house of Lorraine under Francis Stephen.

1799–1814 Tuscany is occupied by Napoleon's troops.

1865–70 Florence becomes the capital of Italy. King Vittorio Emanuele is installed in the Pitti Palace.

1944 On 4 August, Germans blow up all bridges in Florence except the Ponte Vecchio.

1966 The River Arno bursts its banks without warning on 4 November: Florence is flooded, the waters reaching to more than 6m (20ft) in some areas.

1993 The Uffizi Gallery is bombed by the Mafia and five people killed.

2004 Michelangelo's *David* is unveiled after controversial restoration.

2016 Vasari's *Last Supper* (1543), restored after being badly damaged in the 1966 flood, is unveiled in the Museo dell'Opera di Santa Croce.

2019 Despite works upstream to control the flow of the River Arno, water levels reach their highest for 30 years.

2020 Florence closes to visitors as Italy enters quarantine to combat coronavirus.

FAMOUS FLORENTINES

The poet Dante Alighieri, author of the *Divine Comedy*, was born in Florence in 1265. He was exiled from the city in 1302 because of his sympathies with the White Guelphs, and died in 1321.

Michelangelo Buonarroti (1475–1564) created some of his most famous works in Florence, including the sculpture *David*. Born in Caprese, he was buried in Florence's Santa Croce.

Political philosopher Niccolò Machiavelli was born in Florence in 1469.

Galileo Galilei (1564–1642), from Pisa, spent much of his life in Florence as the Medici court mathematician.

From far left: Bust of Cosimo di Giovanni de' Medici and on his horse; Napoleon Bonaparte; Dante Alighieri; fleur-de-lys guild emblem; the defensive Forte di Belvedere

Index

127

Titles in the Series